# FISHING
## FOR THE
# FUTURE

How to Anchor and Grow Your Church
Through the Youngest Generations

*by*
## GARY HAYS

ISBN's:

Hardback: 978-1-965401-83-5
Paperback: 978-1-965401-84-2
eBook: 978-1-965401-85-9

# ENDORSEMENTS

## USA

Over the years, I have observed God using ministry leaders in incredible ways. Gary Hays' leadership strategies have grown churches in 20 nations. With the skill of a surgeon, Gary provides proven practical guidelines, not as theory, but from the experience of a successful practitioner.

Don Argue, Former President of the National
Association of Evangelicals North Central University, and
Northwest University

Not your typical How To Book! Fishing For the Future is packed with stories, Biblical references, short biographies, and current data that combine to give you a fun yet educational ride! Most importantly, it provides the best formula to help ensure the future of your church!

Glenn Burris, President of the International Church of
the Foursquare Gospel (2010 – 2020)

If you care about the future of your church and the next generation, you need to read "Fishing for the Future" by Gary Hays. Just as hunter-gatherers learned to farm and fishermen embraced aquaculture for greater abundance, Hays encourages us to "cultivate" children and youth for vibrant, thriving, and sustainable church communities. Get ready to be inspired!

Rev. Kiha Kimental, Christ-Centered Community
Church, Honolulu

Gary Hays has spent much of his life and leadership helping churches minister to the next generation. His new book, Fishing for the Future, offers ecclesial leaders with tools to effectively empower and release the full potential in the younger generations!!

Rev. Steve Mickel, Northwest District Supervisor, The Foursquare Church

For many years as a lead pastor, I have been focused on growing the church through adults. I had an "aha moment" when Rev. Gary Hays cast the vision for how thinkSMALL's social ministry approach could secure the future of our church. The impact was so profound that we are transitioning our ministry to greater involvement in child evangelism and child protection ministry!

Rev. Alex Chai, Pastor Word of Life Fellowship, Billings, Montana

Fishing For the Future calls us all to see children through God's eyes and as full partners in God's mission. I hope you will treasure this amazing book and allow our Heavenly Father to "capture your heart" for every child - everywhere!

Tom Victor, Director, 2BC World - 2 Billion Children

For those of us who have seen the results, saying yes to Gary Hays' easy-to-read, informative book is one of those "Yes's" that will bring your church to new levels of vitality and longevity!

Rev. Cere Muscarella, Life Foursquare Church, Angleton, TX

ENDORSEMENTS

Fishing for the Future is more than a book—it's a divine invitation and catalyst to revival in the Church. This is a vital blueprint for EVERY leader who longs to see God's vision of a thriving, dynamic, and healthy church come to reality. Gary's captivating storytelling, raw vulnerability, humor, and proven practical strategies kept me fully engaged, turning each chapter into an inspiring journey of discovery. This book is a gift from heaven, a divine tool that will shape and impact generations to come!

Michele Okimura, Executive Director,
Releasing Generations, Author; Dancing with Father

Throughout the many years that I have known Gary, I have been inspired by God's grace in his life to reach and disciple children from some of the hardest-hit, least-reached places on earth. I hope this book will be a blessing to you as he shares insights, heart, and proven wisdom. Gary's stories and anecdotes take this book away from being a mere outline of principles to an inspiring and innovative approach to reaching and discipling children.

Dr. Ted Vail, Senior Vice President of Global Operations
for the Foursquare Church

This book is a must-read for pastors in the "third-third" of their years of service. Leaving a legacy behind involves discipling young leaders who disciple children!

Rev. Jim Hayford,
D.Min Asian Theological Seminary

Fishing for the Future's compelling illustrations, heartfelt stories, inspiring testimonies, and touches of humor will challenge and encourage you to believe that God can use you to do something extraordinary!

Rev. George Butron, Global Prayer Coordinator,
Foursquare Global Ministries

Church leaders, get ready for a transformative journey! In Fishing for the Future, Gary Hays offers a vision-driven roadmap to revitalize your ministry by empowering youth and children. With engaging stories and practical strategies drawn from his global success and unique background in military, business, and ministry leadership, this book is a must-read for securing your church's future!

Dr. Dave Metsker, Fuller Theological Seminary; Professor
Life Pacific College (1993-2007); Editor, Ministry
Training Network

Gary Hays has an amazing passion for Jesus and a remarkable dedication to reaching children worldwide. The fruit of his ministry proves God's hand on his life!

Rev. Craig Langhans, Pastor,
Mission Church, Spokane, WA

This book will be a great help to pastors. It's simple, concise and clear!

Rev. Gary Matsdorf, Ministry Leadership Director/Professor at
New Hope Christian College

## ASIA

I met Rev. Gary in Thailand and was inspired by his passion for discipleship and leadership training. His teaching showed us how to share the Gospel in tough situations and reminded us that even small steps of faith can transform our communities!"

Pastor James, Asia Center Foundation and Cornerstone Community Baptist church in Phuket, Thailand.

thinkSMALL's training was an answer to prayer. It gave us the tools to fight drug addiction and protect our children. Now, through parenting seminars and teen mentorship, God is healing our community and giving our youth hope.

Pastor Todd, A little Hug church in Pattaya, Thailand

I discovered thinkSMALL in Danao, Philippines. I was deeply moved by their passion for empowering local leaders. Their Child Protection training showed me that God uses humble, Spirit-led steps to spark real change! Now, entire families are coming to Christ!

Pastor Kim, Living Word Lion of Judah Danao, Philippines

I first heard about thinkSMALL through a fellow pastor. When I attended their initial workshops, I was struck by how their simple, yet powerful approach resonated with the challenges we face in our country. Gary reminded us that God calls us to be faithful where we are, even when resources are limited.

Denomination President (Restricted Country and Name withheld for security reasons)

For 5 years I have witnessed the power of Pastor Gary's teachings to help churches reach children for Christ in India, Nepal and Bangladesh. These teachings are transforming lives and building an exciting new future for South Asia churches!

Rev. Raj Mondal, Former District Education Coordinator,
Church of the Nazarene, Kolkata District, India

Pastor Gary introduced thinkSMALL to our country, revolutionizing how we reach children. Over 200 churches have been trained in teaching children how to resist drugs and protecting them from trafficking and abuse. As a result, more than 7,000 children have entered discipleship!

Pastor Janak Basnet, Jhapa District, Nepal

As a pastor in Bangkok, I've seen the powerful impact of Pastor Gary's teachings on our ministry and local children. Thanks to thinkSMALL, we now have active children's ministries in two communities—something we couldn't do before. Our church is stronger because of his partnership!

Pastor Sathit Sutancharoen, Our Home Chapel, Bangkok

## AFRICA

Before Pastor Gary's visit, we struggled to evangelize children for Christ. Based on his teachings, 322 churches have been trained, with youth teams reaching children with child protection outreaches. This has resulted in more than 300,000 Burundian children accepting Christ and being discipled in local churches!

Bishop Serges Nsabimana, National Leader,
Foursquare Church, Burundi

Five years ago, Pastor Gary's visit transformed our ministry. His teachings on protecting and reaching children for Christ inspired us—now, over 1,500 children attend our churches in Bujumbura!

Pastor Manirakiza Adolphe, Maranathan Pentecostal church, Bujumbura, Burundi, Africa

Pastor Gary's teachings opened my eyes to the urgency of reaching and protecting children for Christ. His message transformed my ministry, and now over 350 children attend our three local churches. Every pastor needs to learn from his teachings!

Pastor Isaac Bigirimana, Ngozi, Burundi

I've known Pastor Gary for five years—he's the most impactful leader I've ever met. He leads by example, mentors with patience, and inspires others. His guidance has strengthened my leadership and helped raise hundreds of new leaders in our churches.

Xavier Karorero, National Director, New Hope Ministry, Burundi

thinkSMALL came to my church three years ago and has transformed our ministry! Our youth team is now reaching children for Christ and protecting them from trafficking. The greatest blessing is 82 new children who came to Christ and growing in faith! We are so grateful for thinkSMALL and its impact on our community!

Pastor Diecque Bazirutwabo, Methodist Church, Bujumbura

# ACKNOWLEDGMENTS

This book is dedicated to every leader who challenged me, inspired me and guided me through my life.

From my mother (now with the Lord) who held me accountable throughout my early years to my Uncle Finley, who inspired me to follow in his footsteps as a writer. Thanks even to my drill sergeant, whose nose-to-nose intimidation prepared me for service overseas. I am grateful for the wisdom and knowledge pastors, and business leaders have shared with me over the years.

Thanks to Leadership Books' editing, publishing, and design teams for challenging and encouraging me to complete this God-inspired journey.

I am eternally grateful for my wife, Paula. It was her idea to write this book. At first, I resisted, but her encouragement, love, prayers, and laughter always refueled me when I ran on empty. Hon, there will never be another for me.

And especially to Jesus, whose Spirit, Word, and silent whispers have always been with me. I am forever in awe of His grace, patience, and wisdom.

Gary Hays

# TABLE OF CONTENTS

**PART 4: BELOW THE SURFACE: JESUS AND OTHER LEADERS' LESSER-KNOWN SUCCESS STRATEGIES**

# READ THIS FIRST!

We've never met, but I know something about you.

I may be wrong. Let's see…

You are wondering about the long-term future of your church. At least one of these things is happening; Your congregation is aging or declining. Young people seem less interested in attending church. And of the ones who do, only a brave few feel called to ministry. As a result, you are wondering who will lead your church into the future. Am I right?

If so, this book is for you.

You are not alone. Most churches in the Western world are experiencing the same struggles. A ship taking on water has only two options: plug the leak or bail. Tossing water overboard just delays the inevitable. The hole widens, you become exhausted, and your ship sinks. You need solutions to ensure that your boat stays afloat permanently.

I know something else about you. You are busy. You have a lot on your plate aside from a good meal. Weekly staff meetings, administrative tasks, counseling sessions, funerals, weddings, hospital visits, sermon writing, and dealing with employee politics are just a handful of your time-consuming responsibilities. Marriage, parenthood, hobbies, continuing education, Bible reading, and prayer time are all a part of your life puzzle.

You have no time for empty promises, so here is mine. If you are looking for solutions, this book will not waste your time.

*Fishing for the Future* was written for leaders willing to turn around negative trends that threaten the future of their church. The strategies in this book are successful in ministry, sports, government, and business. Most importantly, they are rooted in scripture, and are able to be contextualized for churches in any nation, any culture.

## WHAT YOU WILL LEARN

In this book, you will learn the keys and strategies to help your church get younger, grow bigger, and secure its long-term future—ones that you can implement as soon as you turn the final page. These include:

1. Little-known Biblical Strategies.

    * ...successfully used in religion, sports, business, and government (and how to use them to grow your church)
    * How to customize strategies to fit youth and children.

2. Social Ministry

    * How Jesus and other prominent leaders leveraged it to achieve their mission.
    * Steps to understand the unmet felt needs of your community, opening the door for growth and evangelism.
    * How to influence and gain acceptance in an apathetic or resistant community.
    * Church strategies to lead the fight to eradicate child exploitation (trafficking, social media).

3. Reaching Children

    * Reach and disciple the most open, underutilized generation essential to ensure your survival.

- Learn the keys to keeping them in church through their high school years.
- Prepare them to withstand the cultural attacks on their faith.

4. Reaching Youth

- Create your future leaders through youth-led, cause-driven ministries.
- Learn how to tap into young people's deepest motivations.
- Apply four little-known steps Jesus used to lead and motivate His young team.
- Connect youth to children to build a two-generation force that will grow and secure your church.

5. Preparation and Action Steps

- Write a vision statement that galvanizes and unifies your church.
- Overcome the barriers of antiquated traditions and misguided biases.
- How key leaders apply the concept of pivoting in church and business.
- Set Biblically rooted, practically applied goals that ensure success.
- Outline what is needed to begin immediately.

**Why Should You Listen to Me?**

I became an ordained minister in 2011. But I have never attended a seminary or pastored a church. In fact, before 2005, my background was in military intelligence and as a national manager for a global corporation. The closest I came to Christian ministry was co-directing our church's marriage course with my wife, Paula. We were highly qualified—we had been married for four months. In short, no one else wanted to do it.

In 2004, Paula and I purchased a new house, the home where we expected to live forever. Four months later, God interrupted our plans. One day in my office, I heard Him, a whisper as forceful as a hurricane. "Sell your house! Sell your car! Quit your career! Move to Thailand and advance my Kingdom!" I laughed…He didn't. I said yes. As a military veteran, I know when I've been given an order.

Why Thailand? 96 percent of their residents are Buddhist, 4 percent are Muslim, and less than 1 percent are Christian. The need was clear. I had no idea how to get the job done. And as much as I love the Lord, I would have appreciated more instructions. But He said go. So we went.

Since I was a businessman and entrepreneur, I launched a ministry to help local churches start small enterprises to promote the Gospel and generate church revenue. It was a successful ministry. But it brought more money to the church than people. We needed a new plan.

After five months of frustration and prayer, it hit me. My mistake was in praying for a comfortable strategy rather than the best one. I thought "What if God's strategy had little to do with my background?" I started praying a simple, yet terrifying prayer; "I'll do anything!"

The Lord seemed to respond, "I've been waiting for you to say that!" He led me to a Biblical strategy that inspired my wife and me to create a ministry. We named it thinkSMALL. Eventually, more than 270,000 Thais accepted Christ as Lord in 840 churches. The ministry grew to 20 nations, including Asia, Africa, and the Americas. thinkSMALL's indigenous teams trained over 3,000 churches on how to get younger, grow bigger, and be a more powerful influence on their communities.

By applying the plans and techniques in this book, over 1.4 million people have come to Christ, and over 70 percent have begun formal church discipleship. And we are just getting started.

But let me be clear: These are God's strategies, not mine! That's why they work.

What you learn in this book will work in any ministry, any generation. But if your goal is to grow your church and get younger, direct them toward children, the world's most overlooked, underestimated, vulnerable generation.

## What This Book is Not

*Fishing for the Future* is not a 'get successful with no effort' scheme. Planning, commitment, and action are required. If you are willing to take the steps outlined in this book, your church will expand and become younger. God and your level of commitment will determine how much.

These strategies in this book will work in every nation and every community. They can reverse the trend of a declining church and revitalize a healthy one. They will establish your next generation of leaders, raise a more committed generation of Jesus followers, strengthen your relationship with your community, and ensure long-term sustainable growth for your church!

Your community cannot be transformed without your church. Your church cannot do it without children. Children cannot do it without Jesus.

Let's get started.

# PART 1

# STORM WARNINGS: TRENDS THAT CHALLENGE THE LOCAL CHURCH

I t's time to get out of the foxhole.

I volunteered for the Air Force during wartime, serving four years in military intelligence across the Middle East and Asia.

I had a close friend who was a Marine. John was a terrific guy. He was kind but tough enough to take on any adversary. Obviously, he was a good friend to have. All I had to do was call his name. "Hey John! These guys are trying to fight me!" Here comes John. Problem solved.

One day, he asked me, "Gary, where is the safest place on the battlefield?" I knew it was a trick question.

"I don't know, John. I suppose it is the foxhole?"

"No, you goof! (One of his more enduring names for me) That is the most dangerous place you can be!"

"Why, John?"

"There are two reasons. First, the enemy knows you are hiding in a hole. He calculates your location, signals an armed plane, and, well…you are dead."

"OK. Not a good choice. Where is the safest place on the battlefield, John?"

"Moving toward the enemy! Never remaining in one place for long. Continually changing your position. Zigzagging left and right, but always forward. When you get close enough to fire your shot accurately, you shoot to kill!"

"John, I'm glad I joined the Air Force."

"Gary, you are still a soldier. You might not carry a rifle and grenades. But you chose to join the fight! You need to step up!"

Church leaders, you are in a war much more devious than the ones I engaged. Yours is against the forces of evil that can erode the future of your church, your community and nation. It's time for all of us to step up. It's time to win!

As in the military, the first step in winning a war is to understand the trends and tactics of the enemy. Many of the trends happening around the world are affecting your church. They may seem overwhelming. They may tempt you to find a foxhole in which to hide. Do so at your peril!

Your goal is to grow your church, secure its long-term future, and become a change agent for your community. You need a strategy. The first step is to identify the global and national trends that negatively impact your church. Then you can design a plan to address them.

Chapters 1 and 2 will unveil many of these trends and why you need to pay attention to them: trends such as the growth of multiple religions (including 'no religion') and the reduction of family sizes (and how they affect your church). We will examine the downward trends of church attendance and increased congregation age in the Western World and why it has occurred. We will touch on an issue nearly every pastor is concerned about; the increasing exodus of young people from church.

Paying attention to the warning signs is the first step to victory. Let's do it together.

## CHAPTER 1

# ROUGH WAVES AHEAD: GLOBAL CHANGES IMPACTING YOUR CHURCH!

---

*19"Come, follow me," Jesus said, "and I will send you out to fish for people." (Matthew 4:19)*

---

Why was Jesus so fascinated by fishermen? He clearly had a heart for fishers who toiled day and night through endless waves, tossing their nets without catching a single fish. Ever feel like that? Jesus did...at least sometimes. Your church is a fishing boat. As captain and navigator, you are determined to guide your ship toward the vision God has given you: a sustainable, growing church. How do you achieve it? Outside forces (community apathy or resistance) can be overwhelming, and sometimes intimidating. You have done your best to connect to the needs of your congregation, widened your connection to the local community, added more ministry opportunities, upgraded your worship team, and added espresso to your coffee bar. But your church still falls short of one critical goal: long-term sustainable growth with a younger congregation.

The ones you counted on leading the future of your church sometimes slip out the back door. Some exit to other churches, while some leave the faith entirely. Despite your best efforts, your congregation is aging, and the attendance is inconsistent.

Cultural values are constantly shifting. They present serious threats to the local church. This book will give you the strategies needed to grow, get younger and ensure your future despite them.

Let's revisit the fishing boat analogy. As captain, you've assembled your crew. Your assistant pastor is your First Mate. Officers (elders or pastors) and deckhands (support staff) comprise the rest of your team. Lounging in deck chairs, sipping cool drinks and observing your work are your congregants (just a joke).

As a fisherman, a key goal is to haul as many fish into the boat as possible. The more you catch, the more profitable it will be for everyone, especially for the One who owns the boat.

*6 "He said, 'Throw your net on the right side of the boat and you will find some.' When they did, they were unable to haul the net in because of the large number of fish.* (John 21:6)

The apostles fished throughout the night unsuccessfully. They came to believe there were no fish in the vicinity. Jesus' instructions to them proved different. The issue was not that there were no fish nearby. The problem was they did not know where they were and how to catch them. Successful fishermen prepare well. Before launching, they check the weather for any impending storms. They avoid the worst ones. They can discern which ones are manageable and can be used for an advantage. Rather than push against headwinds, they maneuver their boat to allow the wind to guide them faster to their destination. You can as well.

How do you prepare to sail within the storms of your local community or national culture? Hopefully, you ensure your boat is in good condition, equipped with the best equipment, and not prone to leaks. You study the tides and do research to learn where the hungriest fish gather. You choose your bait carefully. You ideally gather a team of like-minded 'net throwers' to join you on your boat. Perhaps they are named Andrew, Peter, James, and John.

Jesus is the Master Fisherman. However, many leaders are unaware of some of His most effective fishing techniques. This book will guide you to the best methods to 'cast your net', where your biggest harvest lies. Your next generation of leaders will rise as you mobilize youth into leading a dynamic new ministry. And you will discover how to connect with your community's unmet needs, resulting in additional levels of growth.

## THAT'S ONCE

The year was 1881. Tombstone, Arizona was the town 'too tough to die.' Strolling into Tombstone (aptly named) was often a dangerous proposition. The sheriff had banned guns outside the city. The ban did not include rifles, shotguns or other weapons. Inside the town, people were armed. Weak men (and women) dared not spend too much time at the saloon card table.

One day, Marshall Virgil Earp, his brothers and friend Doc Holliday made their mark in American Old West history. Five unruly cowboys were armed and ready for them at the O.K. Corral. It didn't end well for the cowboys. After 30 shots were fired, three of them lay dead. Two ran away.

A few days later a cowboy decided to take a bride. He gathered his drinking buddies at the local church, put a gold ring on his new wife's finger, lifted her onto his horse and rode off. It was to be a long ride; 40 miles to his ranch.

They set off but after about an hour, the horse slipped on a rock, stumbling a bit. The new bride watched her husband lean forward and heard him whisper into the horse's left ear. "That's once."

Further down the trail, the horse, startled by a sleeping rattlesnake, halted. The wife watched her husband lean forward again, whispering to his horse "That's two."

A bit confused but not overly concerned she wrapped her arms tightly around his waist as they continued to ride. Still 20 miles to go.

As they passed through the field, the horse let out a sneeze. The old cowboy pulled back on the reins, causing the horse to stop in its tracks. He gently lifted his wife off the horse.

What happened next is still a legend in Tombstone today.

The cowboy shouted at his horse "That's three!" He lifted his six-gun from its holster and shot the horse dead.

The bride, in disbelief at what she had just witnessed screamed at her new husband "How could you have been so cruel to this innocent animal! I had no idea you were this kind of man! And now, worst of all, you are making us walk 20 miles! You brute!!!"

The old cowboy seemed unfazed. He looked at his bride, leaned over and whispered in her ear, "That's once."

At least from the horse's perspective, paying attention to warnings is often the key to survival.

## THEY NEVER SAW IT COMING

December 26, 2004 changed the course of history in Thailand. Prior to that fateful day, Thais and international visitors played happily on the beach of Phuket Island. Tourists had long dreamed of visiting this sunny paradise on the Andaman Sea, seeking a reprieve from the chilly winters of their Western worlds. Today was a day when Heaven seemed to touch the shore. Gentle waves soothed the warm ivory-colored sand. Children bounced happily on the sand while others built castles or played tag with the water. Swimmers, snorkelers, body surfers, kayakers—they were all there. It was perfect.

Far from shore, a small vibration disturbed a calm sea. No one knew that a magnitude 9 earthquake had just lifted the floor of the Indian Ocean.

The initial waves were small, less than a foot high. Slowly, they picked up size and speed, traveling faster than 500 miles per hour and reaching more than 100 feet high. Their first target? The beaches of Indonesia, killing over 100,000 people.

The tsunami's ravenous appetite continued to grow. It headed straight for the beach of Phuket Island. The first wave landed gently before receding over 1600 feet (the length of 5 football fields). Dead fish lay on the damp sand and intrigued beachgoers who happily gathered them up. A lifeguard screamed "Tsunami!" Few people heard his cry. In the next moment, the ocean exhaled a wave the size of a 7-story building toward shore. It surged forward at the speed of an airliner, increasing in size and roaring toward the astonished crowds. They ran, desperate to avoid certain death. Few survived. One tourist described the devastation this way: "An hour earlier, we were sunbathing with our family outside our hotel. Now everything is gone, including my family. I don't even know where to look."

The tsunami did not finish until it reached 12 nations. Over 230,000 people died, replaced only by broken buildings, demolished trees, and devastated lives. The energy released was equivalent to that of over 20,000 nuclear bombs, each the size of the one dropped on Hiroshima in 1945.

Were there warning signs in advance of this catastrophe? Yes.

Just before 8 a.m., an alarm rang at Hawaii's Pacific Tsunami Warning Center. Seismic signals from stations in Australia showed an underwater earthquake and potential tsunami in the Indian Ocean.

Hawaii responded with frantic calls to India, Sri Lanka, Indonesia, and Thailand. But the calls were misunderstood, ignored, or disbelieved. In Java, Indonesia, seismological equipment sent warnings. Amazingly, the receiving office had yet to install a telephone line.

In Thailand, seismologists had detected the earthquake that stirred the initial wave. Yet, meteorologists couldn't confirm if a tsunami was imminent as there were no tsunami sensors in the ocean. A few of them were concerned that announcing a warning during the tourist season would negatively affect business. The result? Over 5,400 people lost their lives in Thailand. The 2004 tsunami was the deadliest in history, with 227,899 people killed or missing. Approximately 1.7 million people were homeless. The total damage amounted to about 13 billion dollars.

Ignoring warning signals, even for your church, can lead to disaster.

---

"History is a vast early warning system"
—Norman Cousins

---

## OAHU, HAWAII

In November 1941, Army private George E. Elliott, Jr operated a radar unit on the northern tip of Oahu, Hawaii. The SCR-270-B R radar unit was state-of-the-art for its time. Its purpose was to identify and track aircraft movements up to 150 miles away.

He had little idea that a month later he would be at the center of history.

George and his partner, private Joseph Lockhard, were guarding the radar early morning on December 7. The weather was perfect. Only the chill of a Hawaiian winter breeze crawling up Opana Mountain to the radar location disturbed their comfort. George was manning the oscilloscope, watching the screen. Any blip on its screen would signify the movement of planes.

When interviewed years later, George said it was "the biggest blip either of us had ever seen." He called to his partner, "What is this?"

George called the radar plotting station to report the unusual event. Soon, Lt. Kermit Tyler returned the call. Tyler instructed Elliot and Lockhard to ignore the oscilloscope's reading. A dozen American B-17 bombers were due to arrive from San Francisco. "Of course," Tyler thought. "The blip on the screen was them."

The blip was 183 Japanese aircraft headed for Pearl Harbor. Had the radar warning sign been respected, the surprise attack would not have had the devastating effect of 2,403 dead Americans. It may not have prevented the attack, but many heroes would have survived.

Today, Thailand and other Asian nations have early warning technology to signal the impending arrival of tsunamis. Evacuation systems and alarms are in place to allow people ample time to escape the beach before the waves arrive.

Modern military is now equipped with satellite technology to warn of potential enemy attacks. When spotted, officers immediately issue warnings. But warnings are only helpful for those who recognize them and are willing to respond. Ignoring them can be deadly.

Despite the dangers in this world, most of it seems normal and often inspiring. The mailman still comes on time. Neighbors smile at one another (at least occasionally). Babies are born. Families celebrate holidays. We continue to hear inspiring tales of miraculous medical achievements. People willingly volunteer their time, serving others in Godly causes. Martyrs still exist. There is still hope in the world.

Regardless, Satan has secured his place within our nations. And he is not leaving.

## FALLING SHORT: THE GREAT COMMISSION

As Jesus ascended to Heaven, He commanded His followers to go into the world and make disciples of all nations (Matthew 28:19-20, Mark 16:15, Acts 1:8, Luke 14:23).

It seemed impossible. How did His disciples suppress a laugh? If I were in the group, I'd be thinking, "The only one who can pull this off is heading out of town!"

There is more evangelism in the world than any time in history. Satellite technology, online programming, video, music, and movies reach every corner of the world. Television stations broadcast Christian messages and sermons unendingly. The Bible has been translated (in whole or part) into 3,658 languages.[1]

People are coming to Christ faster than at any time in history. However, we've lost ground. Today (2024), only 31.6 percent of the global population identifies as Christian,[2] down from 35 percent in 1900.[3] It continues to decline. The global population is accelerating faster than evangelism.

**Percentage of Christians (vs Global Population)**

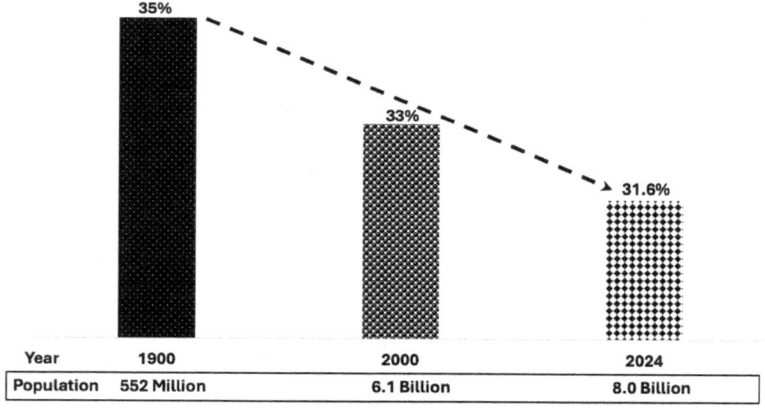

| Year | 1900 | 2000 | 2024 |
|---|---|---|---|
| Population | 552 Million | 6.1 Billion | 8.0 Billion |

[1] Wycliffe Global Alliance, 2023 Global Scripture Access; https://www.wycliffe.net/resources/statistics2023/

[2] Statista, Share of global population affiliated with major religious groups in 2022, by religion; https://www.statista.com/statistics/374704/share-of-global-population-by-religion/

3 Pew Research Center, Pew 2013 Number of Christians Rises, But Their Share of World Population Stays Stable; www.pewresearchcenter.com

The call of the Great Commission is as relevant today as it was 2,000 years ago. But we will continue to fall behind unless we implement faster ways to bring people to Christ. This is particularly true in the Western world; While Christianity has surged in Latin America, Africa, and Asia, it has slowed in North America, Europe, Australia, and other Western countries.

---

*"The era of Western Christianity has passed within our lifetimes, and the day of Southern Christianity is dawning."*
—Philip Jenkins, The Next Christendom

---

## GLOBAL TRENDS AFFECTING THE CHURCH

1. The Growth of Other Religions

People around the world are becoming more religious. That is a good thing. But what religions are they choosing? Pew Research conducted a study in 2022 comparing multiple religions and projecting their growth (or decline) until the year 2050. The results were startling. Hinduism, Buddhism, and folk religions are expected to decline globally as a percentage of the world population. Judaism and Christianity will remain roughly at their current levels. The growth of Islam, however, is accelerating as the fastest-growing religion in the world, nearly matching the global population of Christians by 2050.

Christianity is growing fastest in African nations south of the Sahara Desert, representing 40 percent of the world's Christian population. But this is also the region where Islam is spreading most rapidly, primarily because of large family sizes.[4]

---

[4] Pew Research Center, Key Findings From the Global Religious Futures Project; https://www.pewresearch.org/religion/2022/12/21/key-findings-from-the-global-religious-futures-project/

## 2. A Declining Number of Adult Christians:

In 46 surveyed nations, including the USA and Canada, young adults are less likely than older adults to affiliate with any religion.[5] If the trend continues, there will eventually be fewer Christians to replace those who die from old age.

## 3. The Growth of The '"Nones"':

In the Western World, the chief force against Christianity is the growing popularity of no religion at all. I call them the "Nones."

The "Nones" describe themselves as 'atheist, agnostic, or nothing in particular.' About 24 percent of Western Europeans and Americans identify as "Nones." What may surprise you is that 24 percent of the American 'Nones" claim to believe in God.[6] They sense someone, or something is 'out there' somewhere. Perhaps someone planted a seed in their spirit when they were children or a feeling they cannot shake. Whatever the reason, it is a step in the right direction. Western European "Nones" are far less likely to believe in God, with only between 1 percent to 3 percent proclaiming that belief.[7]

Because of the expanding influence of secular-based cultures, social media, and supportive governments, the "Nones" will continue to grow…unless the church turns it around.

## AMERICA

The Great Commission stirred America's first nationwide spiritual movement. Leaders such as Jonathan Edwards and George Whitfield

---

[5] Pew Research Center, Key Findings From the Global Religious Futures Project; https://www.pewresearch.org/religion/2022/12/21/key-findings-from-the-global-religious-futures-project/

[6] Pew Research Center, Religious Landscape Study; https://www.pewresearch.org/dataset/pew-research-center-2014-u-s-religious-landscape-study/

7 Pew Research Center, Being Christian in Western Europe; https://www.pewresearch.org/religion/2018/05/29/being-christian-in-western-europe/

launched the Great Awakening. Their goal was to reawaken complacent church members. Whitfield became immensely popular, traveling and preaching across several colonies, even becoming close friends with Benjamin Franklin. The American movement revitalized Christianity during its decline and introduced principles that shaped American culture and paved the way for a new nation.

The Second Great Awakening began in New England and spread to the Midwest around 1800. It focused primarily on reaching non-Christians. Much of the evangelism was by country pastors or "circuit riders" who traveled on horseback from town to town.

From the 1850s to the early 20th Century, the Third Great Awakening inspired evangelists to ride horseback to townships and cities. People gathered in tent services, town halls, or parks to hear these missionaries proclaim the Gospel of Jesus. Local church pastors, Christian volunteer organizations, and a mobilized population ignited and fanned a spiritual flame nationwide.

People were jammed into church pews only to be outnumbered by those standing outside attempting to get in.

If only it were that way today.

Since the 70s, the percentage of adult American Christians has fallen while the percentage of "'Nones'" has escalated.[8] In 1970, 90 percent of Americans identified as Christian. That number dropped to 64 percent in 2020.[9]

---

[8] Pew Research Center, Key Findings From the Global Religious Futures Project; https://www.pewresearch.org/religion/2022/12/21/key-findings-from-the-global-religious-futures-project/

[9] Pew Research Center, Modeling the Future of Religion in America; https://www.pewresearch.org/religion/2022/09/13/modeling-the-future-of-religion-in-america/

## EUROPE

My wife, Paula, and I visited the Netherlands recently. Although a beautiful nation, there was little visible Christian presence. Many churches have closed or renovated to become restaurants or bars. Some have become mosques.

While in Amsterdam, we attended a Sunday service. The church was beautiful. Built in the 1800s, it stood as a shining beacon of God. The golden-trimmed stained-glass windows depicted scenes of Jesus and His apostles, filling the sanctuary with holiness. As we entered, we estimated the room could seat 1,000 congregants. When the service began, 12 older adults were in the pews—no one else.

After the service, we visited the pastor. He reflected on a time early in his career. "The pews were full. There was life in this church." His eyes dropped. "Not anymore. My country has thrown away God."

In 1900, 95 percent of the Netherlands' population identified as Protestant or Catholic. In 2022, only 32 percent of Dutch residents are Christian.

The North Sea separates the Netherlands and the United Kingdom, where young people increasingly leave the church. Lord Carey, the former Archbishop of Canterbury, states: "As I have repeated many times in the past, we are one generation away from extinction. We must give compelling reasons to young people why the Christian faith is relevant to them."

Forces that threaten Christianity continue to spread across the Western world like a relentless disease. Atheism, secular humanism, agnosticism, other religions and the 'Nones' are no longer merely a threat. They are winning the day.

Pseudoscience and social media have combined to influence the younger generations. Outside forces are shifting modern culture and eroding the desire to live for a higher purpose than oneself.

In the U.K., roughly 6 percent of people attend church weekly. Are the trends of Western European Christianity a warning sign for America? American leaders, pay note: Unless you take immediate and decisive action to disciple an increased number of youth and children, you will suffer the same fate.

## WHAT IS NEEDED

*"Men have forgotten God; That's why all this has happened."*
—Alexander Solzhenitsyn

Alexander Solzhenitsyn was born into a Christian family that belonged to the Russian Orthodox Church. While still young, he became a Marxist and atheist. In 1945, he was forced into a Russian gulag for the crime of criticizing the government. While in camp, he regained His faith. He stood his ground against the Communist government by writing books that criticized the Soviet Union's human rights abuses.

Solzhenitsyn was doing what the Soviet Union was most afraid of--drawing a crowd. Thousands listened to him and read his books. They eventually deported him to West Germany, afraid that returning him to the gulag would stir up his supporters. He eventually moved to the United States. After several years, his Russian citizenship was taken away. He continued to write books as a stand against his former nation, eventually rewarded with a Nobel Prize for Literature. Shortly before the Soviet Union's dissolution, the government reinstated his citizenship. He lived his remaining days as a hero in his original nation.

Alexander Solzhenitsyn not only stood his ground. His shrewd aggression was his best defense and his eventual victory. Today, more than ever, we need Christian men and women to gather the courage to take a stand for Christ despite resistant or apathetic cultures. How about you?

Some critics think that Christianity's decline in the Western world isn't necessarily a bad thing. They see it as a sign of evolving social customs and an evolution toward more religious diversity. They believe that developing other belief systems fosters inclusiveness and tolerance in society. They maintain that the decline in Christianity is a natural shift in an enlightened, globalized, and interconnected world rather than a sign of moral decay. They are, of course, wrong.

## HOPE

Despite the downward trends, there is hope. Western nations are experiencing a rise in spiritual hunger. The Barna Group's 2022 survey polled adult Americans and found the following results:

1. 80 percent believe the world has a spiritual or supernatural dimension.
2. 77 percent believe in a higher power.

3.  44 percent are more open to God than before the COVID pandemic.

4.  74 percent say they want to grow spiritually![10]

Since American and Western European cultures are relatively similar, Europeans should also find some hope in these results.

A new question arises: "Is the church prepared for this new harvest opportunity?"

## OVERCOMING YOUR GOLIATH

---

[16] *"Look, I am sending you out as sheep among wolves.*
*So be as shrewd as snakes and harmless as doves"*
(Matthew 10:16).

---

It's not enough to have a winning vision. You need a winning strategy.

When David squared off with Goliath, victory seemed impossible. Only one person gave him a chance: David.

Malcolm Gladwell wrote about it in his book *David and Goliath.*

"Ancient armies had three kinds of warriors. The first was cavalry—armed men on horseback or in chariots. The second was infantry—foot soldiers wearing armor and carrying swords and shields. The third were projectile warriors, or what today would be called artillery: archers and, most important, slingers. Slingers had a leather pouch attached on two sides by a long strand of rope. They would put a rock or a lead ball into the pouch, swing it around in increasingly wider and faster circles, and then release one end of the rope, hurling the rock forward. Slinging took an

---

[10]  *2023 Rising Spiritual Openness in America*

extraordinary amount of skill and practice. But in experienced hands, the sling was a devastating weapon. An experienced slinger could kill or seriously injure a target at a distance of up to two hundred yards…. Imagine standing before a Major League Baseball pitcher as he aims a baseball at your head. That's what facing a slinger was like—only what was being thrown was not a ball of cork and leather but a solid rock. And projectile warriors were deadly against infantry, because a big lumbering soldier, weighed down with armor, was a sitting duck for a slinger launching projectiles from a hundred yards away. Goliath is heavy infantry. He thinks he will be engaged in a duel with another heavy infantryman. When he says, "Come to me, that I may give your flesh to the birds of the heavens and the beasts of the field," the key phrase is "come to me." He means come right up to me so we can fight at close quarters."

David was courageous and ready to confront Goliath with an unconventional weapon.—the sling. Traditional armor was insufficient.

David's approach was speed, refusing to be hindered by the weight of a breastplate and sword. Unlike conventional wisdom, he planned to run directly toward Goliath, darting left and right to avoid the giant. Once close enough to load the stone, he'd whip it around several times at increasing velocity and let it fly…straight to the big man's forehead! Whack!

According to experts, if David threw a stone from 35 meters (about 40 yards) at an experienced slinger's speed, it would have traveled at 34 meters per second and hit Goliath's head with enough force to penetrate his skull.

"You come against me with sword and spear and javelin," David shouts to Goliath, "but I come against you in the name of the Lord!

Robert Dohrenwend writes, "Goliath had as much chance against David as any Bronze Age warrior with a sword would have had against an opponent armed with a .45 automatic pistol."

Like David, we must confront the enemy head-on, using less traditional weapons of war. It is time to win back our nations by raising a new army of overlooked and underestimated soldiers: the children.

## KEEP IN MIND:

1. Pay Attention to The Global Trends: The percentage of Christians continues to decline compared to global population growth.

2. Identify the Real Issues: Recognize that the opportunities for church growth are less about programs and facilities than about increasing ministries for youth and children.

3. Be Open To Fresh Strategies: God often delivers success through unexpected, overlooked, and underestimated methods.

In the next chapter, we'll study three ominous tides that affect nearly every church. You will undoubtedly recognize them. Let's cast off!

## CHAPTER 2

# BATTLING THE TIDES: THREE COMMON THREATS TO THE LOCAL CHURCH

*"Watch out! Be on your guard!"*
—Luke 12:15

"My church had more red flags than a Chinese
military parade."
—anonymous pastor

"Writing sermons is simple nowadays," the pastor said. "In the past, I was concerned how my message resonated with three different generations. Now, with two of them gone, I can just focus on the "40-year-olds!"

In this chapter, we will examine three trends that threaten churches worldwide: Aging, declining congregations, and young people leaving the church. If any of these are occurring in your church, look out!! The future of your church is at risk.

It didn't begin this way.

## THE BOSTON LATIN SCHOOL

Boston Latin School was founded in 1635. It is the oldest school in America. The Reverend John Cotton, who left England as a Puritan to lead the Boston Church, was its inspiration. Educating and equipping students to become influential leaders in their communities was a hallmark of the school. Teachings included Biblical teaching and prayer.

The school regularly gave rise to well-known individuals in the country, especially in religion, politics, business, and the arts. Famous graduates included Samuel Adams, Cotton Mather, John Hancock, and Ralph Waldo Emerson.

The Boston Latin School rose to prominence in the field of education. It served as a blueprint for others, and Alumni, rooted in Christian education, have contributed to shaping American values and laws for over 400 years. Schools such as the Boston Latin School, in concert with local churches, produced the nation's most prominent business leaders who financially blessed their communities in multiple ways: contributions to charities, hospitals, Christian organizations, and schools. Yes, there were a few whose greed got the better of them, but most leaders rooted in Christian education shared generously.

## JOHN D ROCKEFELLER

John D Rockefeller was an example of Christian generosity, perhaps the best in history. Born in Richford, New York, his father was a 'pitchman,' traveling throughout the country selling elixirs such as cures for cancer to anyone gullible enough to believe him. He was a rascal. His mother, Eliza, however, was a devout Christian, teaching him the scriptures and a lesson that carried him the rest of his life. "From the beginning, I was trained to work, to save, and to give."

At 16, J.D. got his first job as a bookkeeper. He spent 10 cents on a red notebook, which he kept the rest of his life. He noted all his expenditures in the notebook, including his charitable giving. "When I was only making a dollar a day," Rockefeller recalled, "I was giving away five, ten, or twenty-five cents." His initial donations were small but well-meaning. He supported his local Baptist church causes, encompassing the Five Points mission, the Mite society, and foreign missions. He even documented giving 10 cents to a poor woman within his church.

Rockefeller read the Bible daily, attended weekly prayer meetings, and conducted Bible studies with his wife. God blessed him with a talent for business and a discipline that led him to one day become the wealthiest and most generous person of his time. By age 53, he met his goal of giving away at least 1 million dollars a year to Christian and other charitable causes, including efforts to rebuild southern states devastated by the Civil War. He contributed millions to high schools and colleges. Rockefeller established medical schools in 21 major international cities. His foundation chartered ships to deliver relief aid to war-torn nations in World War I, and to assist in the removal of Jewish scientists from Nazi Germany. Perhaps his most significant victory came in health care. Rockefeller funded the research and development of a vaccine to end yellow fever, commonly known as "the terror of the Western Hemisphere."

In his lifetime, he gave away an estimated 530 million dollars, equivalent to approximately 14 billion dollars in 2024! J.D. Rockefeller, reflecting on his life at age 86, wrote the following words:

"I was early taught to work as well as play,

My life has been one long, happy holiday;

Full of work and full of play—

I dropped the worry on the way—

And God was good to me every day."

At age 97, his final words were 'raise me a little higher.' God certainly did.

## ROBERT GILMOUR LETOURNEAU

Robert Gilmour LeTourneau was born in Richford, Vermont, in 1988. At age 14, he completed the 6th grade and quit school to go to work, as did 96 percent of children aged 12 and older at the time.

He soon arrived in Portland, Oregon, working as an ironworker apprentice before moving to San Francisco and becoming a welder. Times were tough. So, he also took work as a woodcutter, bricklayer, farmhand, miner, and carpenter's laborer. While some considered him unstable, each skill would pay dividends in his later life.

When he was 21, he completed a correspondence course on mechanics. He then purchased a motorcycle, disassembled the engine, and put it back together in a day. He loved speed—so much so that he injured his neck racing his car, which disqualified him from serving in World War I.

In debt and broke, he took a job leveling land for a wealthy rancher. That is when his life changed. Robert spent the next few years working in road construction, focusing on inventions that improved tractors with earthmoving blades.

Robert invented machines that were beyond the capabilities of regular men. He invented and designed the Electric Wheel, a motorized tire that makes machinery movement easier, along with many other inventions.

Despite the Great Depression, Robert became one of the wealthiest people in America. He interpreted his financial success as a gift from God, compelling him to give away 90 percent of his income to Christian causes.

In his final years, Robert Gilmour LeTourneau focused on ministry, spreading his message of generosity to Christian business leaders worldwide.

Where are the John D. Rockefellers and Robert Gilmour LeTourneau of today? Many of them are still with us.

Blake Mycoskie, the founder of TOMS Shoes, established the "One for One" program, which donates one pair of shoes for every one sold. His compassion has benefitted needy children around the world.

David and Barbara Green, the founders of Hobby Lobby, donate millions to Christian causes, including launching the Bible Museum in Washington, D.C.

Sam Walton, the founder of Wal-Mart, and his family started the Walton Family Foundation. Their massive donations to education, conservation, and community development have impacted millions.

Where are the great Christian business leaders of today? Many. We need more.

## A MONK'S LAMENT

In 1209, St. Francis of Assisi founded the Franciscan order. Young men of the Catholic faith devoted themselves to a life of poverty, prayer, and service to others. One day, God called a young Italian to join a monastery in the breathtaking region of Tuscany. The moment he arrived at the home, he was filled with joy. The building was in a lush, green valley enveloped by rolling lime-colored hills, olive plantations, and vineyards.

In addition to daily prayers, the monastery had only one strict rule: every monk took a vow of silence and was only allowed to speak two words per year.

This was no problem for the young monk. He was not much of a talker anyway. He slept nightly on a straw mat, performed his duties well, and prayed fervently.

After 1 year, he visited the Abbot to say his two words.

"What would you like to say, my son?"

He looked up at the abbot and answered, "Terrible food."

The abbot nodded and sent him on his way.

One year later, the young monk returned.

Invited to speak, he grumbled in frustration, "Hard floor!"

The abbot shook his head in disappointment, sending the young monk back to his room. On the anniversary of his 3rd year, he didn't even wait for the abbot's permission to speak. He locked eyes with him and shouted at the top of his lungs, "I quit!!!

The abbot responded, "Well, I'm not surprised. For 3 years, all I've ever heard you do is complain!"

## WHAT IS HAPPENING TO THE LOCAL CHURCH?

Pastor Michael was the senior pastor of a thriving church, the personification of a 'happy warrior.' On the day we spoke, something seemed different. There was a subtle shift in the tone of his voice. It was regret.

As far as I knew, the local community loved his church. His reputation was spotless. The church worked with local schools, visited retirement homes, and even provided hospice care.

But as many of his congregation aged into retirement (and fixed incomes), donations decreased. The church council decided to act.

Their plan was to invest into programs that would attract more adults to church. With money saved for emergency purposes, they remodeled classrooms in preparation for new ministry programs (marriage classes, family counseling, and drug/alcohol rehabilitation). They spent money on promotional events, even paying for professional speakers.

It began well. People donated money to attend the classes. But in a few months, the 'newness' of these programs wore off. Attendance dropped. So did donations. For every dollar the church invested in new ministries, only about 50 cents came back.

Youth and children's ministries paid the biggest price, as youth were squeezed into smaller rooms to accommodate the new adult classes. The church also reassigned half of the children's teachers to new roles, frustrating the parents. Some responded by leaving the church. "Gary, it turned out that we barely maintained the present while losing our future."

## THREE KEY THREATS TO THE LOCAL CHURCH

Three indicators suggest that your church's future may be at risk. They are:

1. an aging congregation;

2. a declining attendance, and/or;

3. young people leaving the church.

You can definitely steer through these challenging waters! The first step is to discover what's causing the turbulence.

## AN AGING CONGREGATION

The average age of the typical church attendee is increasing. People are living longer, while young people are leaving. Almost half the congregation in Protestant churches is over 65.[11]

Senior pastors, too, are getting older. According to the Barna Group, "In 2022, only 16 percent of Protestant senior pastors are 40 years old or younger, and the average age among pastors is 52."[12]

Another factor is family size. Parents in the United States are choosing to have fewer children. In 1960, the average American family included 2.3 children. In 2023, that number dropped about 20 percent to 1.9 children.[13] Over the same period, the average age women marry rose from 21 to 28.

Reasons include time, money, and cultural values. For many women, career demands clash with the time required to raise additional children. The increasing expense of raising children influences parents to have fewer children. Western culture plays a part as small families are increasingly more valued. Some view having children as restricting their freedom to enjoy hobbies or entertainment.

---

[11] Lifeway Research; U.S. congregations are increasingly small, while U.S. churchgoers are increasingly headed toward larger churches.

[12] Barna Research, The Pastoral Succession Crisis Is Only Getting More Complicated; https://www.barna.com/research/pastoral-succession/

[13] Statista; Average number of own children under 18 in families with children in the United States from 1960 to 2023. https://www.statista.com

Religious choices can affect family size as well. Latter-Day Saints and Muslims have the largest households, with an average of 2.8 children per family. Christians follow with about 2.1 children per family, and Jewish families average 1.9 children. (Whatever happened to the call to "be fruitful and multiply" in Genesis 1:28?)

Fewer children in Christian households lead to an older average family age. Christian families are the oldest of all religious people in the United States. According to Pew Research 2023, "The average aged U.S. Christian is 43, compared with an average age of 33 among the unaffiliated and 38 among people of other religions."[14]

If you want your church to get younger, act now. Waiting for Christian families to have more children is a fool's game! The clock is ticking.

## A DECLINING ATTENDANCE

There are approximately 380,000 churches in the United States. Between 2019 and 2023, the median church attendance declined from 69 to 65 people (Gallup). Roughly 20 percent of Americans attend church every week, and each church experiences fewer than ten spiritual conversions per year.

## THE EXODUS OF YOUNG PEOPLE

1962 was a pivotal year in the fight for religious freedom in the school system. The New York Board of Regents had approved a prayer for its public schools. A legal battle ensued until it reached the United States Supreme Court. The Court ruled that the prayer violated the First Amendment by forcing an establishment of religion. It all began with a letter.

---

[14] Pew Reseach Group; https://www.pewresearch.org/religion/2022/09/13/how-u-s-religious-composition-has-changed-in-recent-decades/

In 1800, the Congregationalist denomination was the largest in Connecticut. Most government leaders were Congregationalists, making the smaller denominations nervous. They feared the state government would soon announce Congregationalism as the official state religion.

Baptist representatives from 23 churches met in Danbury, Connecticut. They hoped to compel their state to abolish all laws establishing a state religion. But they needed support, so they did the unthinkable: They wrote to President Thomas Jefferson.

They could not have sent the letter to a more receptive person. Jefferson had survived a bloody yet successful seven-year war against England for one purpose: to allow Americans the freedom to determine their own destiny rather than having it determined for them.

On December 20, 1787, Jefferson wrote to James Madison, suggesting that he add a bill of rights to the United States Constitution to safeguard citizens from government interference. The first right he requested was "freedom of religion." The Bill of Rights was officially added to the Constitution in 1791.

Jefferson was personally interested in allowing religious freedom. His religious beliefs differed from traditional Christianity. He greatly respected Jesus' moral teachings but struggled to believe in the supernatural. He even constructed his own Bible. He painstakingly cut and glued Jesus' teachings from the King James Bible into a book he named "The Life and Morals of Jesus of Nazareth." The book is at the National Museum of American History in Washington, D.C.

Jefferson received the Danbury Baptists letter on December 30, 1801. Two days later, he wrote, "Legislature should 'make no law respecting an establishment of religion, or prohibiting the free exercise thereof, thus building a wall of separation between Church and State." It became not only a victory for the Danbury Baptists, but the

Supreme Court later utilized his phrase "wall of separation" to emphasize a clear division between church and government.

Sadly, in 1962, lawyers persuaded the Supreme Court to use Jefferson's phrase, even though it was not written in the Constitution. This act ended Christian expression in public schools. In 1963, the Supreme Court took it further, prohibiting Bible readings in public schools. The struggle to protect the free expression of religion in public spaces continues.

The removal of religion from public schools left a void. It was filled with a secular "if it feels good, do it" philosophy. Secularism and religion have been at war ever since.

Middle school-aged children are increasingly leaving church. We assume that they will eventually return, yet only 30 percent do.[15] Churches that fail to nurture and solidify children's faith risk losing them forever.

As church congregations age and decline in size, with young people leaving and families becoming smaller, many churches face an uncertain future. Is yours among them?

## KEEP IN MIND:

1. Church Congregations Are Aging. Smaller families, longer life expectancies, and a lack of child evangelism are key contributors.

2. Church Congregation Sizes Are Decreasing: Other religious options, the exodus of young people, and the lack of effective evangelism strategies contribute to this crisis.

---

[15] Lifeway Research, Most Teenagers Drop Out of Church When They Become Young Adults; https://research.lifeway.com/2019/01/15/most-teenagers-drop-out-of-church-as-young-adults/

3. The Church Youth Population is Decreasing: Young people are increasingly drawn to secular options and away from 'traditional' churches.

There is no greater power than a Jesus-centered church on the move! For almost 2,000 years, local churches have been the primary drivers of compassion and transformation within nations. Churches continue to be God's most powerful messengers of hope. In the next chapter, we will navigate the transformative power and endless potential for churches of all sizes. Hoist the sails!

# PART 2

# ANCHORS OF IMPACT: THE VITAL ROLE OF A MOBILIZED LOCAL CHURCH

Nothing is more effective than a spirit-led church.

It reads like a cliche. The problem with cliches is that, despite being true, the more we repeat them, the less impact they have. Take these, for example:

- Every cloud has a silver lining.
- It goes without saying (so why waste your time saying it?).
- There are plenty more fish in the sea.
- Children are the future.
- Don't judge a book by its cover (unless it's the Bible).
- Grab the bull by the horns (this one might be the dumbest. Why would I want to clasp onto a raging bull's horns?).

Again, there is nothing more impactful than YOUR spirit-led church. Let's not make this a cliche.

Chapters Three and Four explain why the local church can be the greatest weapon against social problems such as drug use and trafficking.

Chapters Five and Six teach you to navigate storms with a clear vision, measure your current position against your goals, set achievable targets, and avoid underwater hazards.

Regardless of its size, your church is capable of more than you ever imagined.

## CHAPTER 3

# NETTING CHANGE: THE POWER OF THE LOCAL CHURCH

*"In the world, you will have tribulation. But take heart; I have overcome the world."*
—John 16:33

"Only Christians, armed with the Word and Spirit, planning and working to spread the kingdom and righteousness of Christ, can transform a nation as well as a neighborhood......"
—Timothy J. Keller

While ministering in Thailand, I heard a story from one of our leaders. It was so unbelievable that, until I verified it, I was sure he made it up.

In a small, traditional Buddhist village in Eastern Thailand, a pastor dreamed of planting a church. The villagers were ardent devotees of Buddha, as well as several Hindu gods. They firmly believed that the only way to lose the protection of their gods was if Jesus was present.

The locals perceived Jesus as offensive to their gods (they were right). Each time the pastor mentioned his church-building plans, they threatened him. One day, the pastor went hiking in the nearby hills. He parked his motorcycle and wandered into the forest, greeted by the fragrant scent of teak, the sight of multi-colored butterflies, and the gentle sound of a distant waterfall. While he strolled along the path, his mind wandered, barely noticing the rustling in the branches above him. A python weighing over 100 pounds suddenly dropped from the tree. Its 10-foot-long body began wrapped around him and squeezed. He struggled to break free, but the snake's grip tightened. Fighting to recapture his breath he wobbled to his feet. He staggered down the path to his motorcycle with the python still coiled tightly around his body. He pulled back the throttle and roared his engine down the road, screaming for help in front of stunned villagers. They quickly sprang into action, grabbing their knives, slicing the snake until it shook loose from the pastor's body.

They stared at each other in disbelief and came to this conclusion: The Christian God was warning them of impending doom unless they allowed a church in their community!

A quaint little church opened a month later.

## MARDI GRAS FOR THE HOMELESS

Nothing turns on a city like Mardi Gras in New Orleans! It begins the day before the religious 'Season of Lent.' For two months, fun-loving people pack the streets. 19 parades happen between January and March in the French Quarter, Uptown, and other locations. Dixieland Jazz music vibrates on Bourbon Street as people walk shoulder to shoulder with other partygoers. Musicians, jugglers, and mimes perform on every street corner. For some, it's a nonstop party. For others, sleep is a distant memory.

In 2019, Grace Fellowship Church held a meeting to plan how to use Mari Gras to bless the community. Recognizing the plight of the city's homeless, they constructed a plan: Mardi Gras for the Homeless! Their goal was simple: to unite the church and community to ease suffering and bring people closer to Christ.

The church collaborated with homeless shelters and organizations in the area. Unified, they entered the surrounding area to seek homeless people and invite them to a Mardi Gras event.

The church urged other churches, businesses, and community members to join its cause. Each organization prepared by collecting clothing, toiletries, and nonperishable food to distribute during the event.

The festival began on January 6. Church members organized stations in multiple locations, including the parade routes and areas near homeless communities. They provided hot meals, haircuts, and warm clothes. They also distributed blankets, chairs, and snacks near the parade route.

The "Mardi Gras for the Homeless" event turned out to be an incredible success, bringing together their community in a vibrant celebration of compassion and support!. The local media picked up the story for the local news. Grace Fellowship Church gained a new moniker; 'the church with a heart.' The spirit of the church was revitalized. Grace Fellowship Church's creative approach to blessing their community during Mardi Gras not only transformed the lives of those in need; it helped the church grow in size and influence in the city. Their compassion for the homeless, coupled with a unique strategy grew their church and the Kingdom of God. It sounds like something Jesus would do!

# THE POWER OF THE LOCAL CHURCH

---

*"I'm convinced that God's eternal purpose to change the world is through His churches. They were planned and purposed by God."*
—Henry Blackaby

---

Youth to pastor: How did you know you wanted to be a pastor? Did Jesus come to you?

Pastor: Well, He did in many ways, son.

Child: But did you see him?

Pastor: Not exactly.

Child: But you're working for Him.

Pastor: Well, yes.

Child: Do you get paid for it?

Pastor: Well, a bit. But it's more a payment of a spiritual kind, son. You are asking some interesting questions. Do you think you might be called to ministry, son?

Child: I don't think so. I don't think I could work for someone I'd never met and not get paid for it.

## THE CHURCH: WHERE WOULD THE WORLD BE WITHOUT IT?

The Christian Church has been the chief force for good in human history. For over 2,000 years, Christian churches have provided the world with people compelled to serve communities in every nation. There's no nation, despite its dangers, where you cannot find Christian missionaries demonstrating a two-handed ministry, one hand reaching out with compassion and the other with the Gospel.

For over 2,000 years, denominations, local churches, missionaries, Christian nonprofit organizations, and volunteers have donated billions of dollars to improve world conditions. Even during the most challenging economic times, the Christian world continues its generosity to benefit others. In America, Christians provide 70 percent of the budgets for nonprofit organizations. Globally, Christians are the primary global funders to help struggling people of other faiths, not as a matter of conversion but of compassion. In the fight against world poverty, Christian believers donate more money than the United States government.

In the 1960s, Seattle, Washington's principal contributor to the economy was the Boeing Company, the world's largest aerospace company. In 1970, Boeing made a major miscalculation. They had gambled on a project called the Supersonic Transport (SST). It was a revolutionary design. Boeing planned to build a plane that would hold 275 passengers and fly at the incredible speed of over 2,000 miles per hour!

In the aviation industry, delays and redesigns can slow the process down. By 1969, Boeing found itself two years behind schedule. They laid off 12,000 workers despite standing orders for 122 SSTs. Finally, in 1970, the orders stopped. Already a billion dollars in debt (from financing the original 747 airplanes), it became clear: No one would loan them additional money for the SSTs. The company slashed about 65 percent of hourly workers, engineers, scientists, office staff, and managerial jobs. A billboard on the outskirts of town read, "Will the last person leaving Seattle turn out the lights?"

Eventually, Boeing was saved, and Seattle survived. Whereas Boeing was the economic lifeblood of Seattle, your church is the spiritual lifeblood of your community. If you remove the spiritual root of your community, you remove all that matters.

## THE RESILIENT CHURCH

In 1954, Laos gained complete independence from France and became a constitutional monarchy. Although the country was primarily Buddhist, Christian churches survived. In 1975, the Lao People's Front seized power and replaced the monarchy with a communist government. One of its first acts was to close the churches and make public evangelism a crime.

The government hoped that closing church buildings would force Christians to cease worshiping. They did not expect Lao Christians to simply move their worship into homes and secret meeting places! The 'invisible' church became a greater threat to the government than the 'visible' one. So, they changed their approach. They permitted a few denominations to hold services in public churches so long as the sermons did not criticize the government. Lao government representatives would attend church services to ensure churches comply.

What about other atheistic nations? In Communist China, the underground church is far more extensive than the government-approved church. Less than 30 million Chinese Christians attend officially sanctioned churches. However, the underground church has roughly 85 million congregants. Laos, China, and other restrictive nations eventually conceded, allowing above-ground churches. Their lesson? The Christian God is not bound by brick and mortar but thrives within the hearts of His people.

1963 was a pivotal year in the United States. John F. Kennedy, the 35th president, was shot and killed in Dallas, Texas. The culture was changing as prayer and Bible reading became prohibited in schools. Pastor Greg Laurie recounts: "... things had gotten so bad in our nation, Time magazine asked this question on their cover, 'Is God dead?' Coincidence? Riots in the streets, political and racial division continued to explode. Talk of revolution was in the air. And God sent one. It was not a moral revolution. It was not a political revolution. Time declared it 'The Jesus Revolution.' It was a full-blown spiritual awakening. We need to pray for another one to happen soon."

It's time for another. Your church and others like yours are the keys to making it happen.

## THE BATTLE IS ON

How is the enemy working today? By targeting the young. His weapons are a reshaped culture, reformed education, and pseudoscience. His goal is to seduce children into a destructive worldview. He is redefining godly words such as love, tolerance, and acceptance to fit an unholy agenda. People leading this movement are true believers, the victims of indoctrination through educational, political, entertainment, and media leaders. They, too, were previously taught to believe these lies. Where we are today has been a long time coming. At the root, this is a spiritual war—one that we need to win.

---

"It is the hearts of men that for better or worse change
the course of human history, not the man-made
organs of government."
—Charles W. Colson, Born Again

---

Crime, sexual immorality, drugs, and other sins are only symptoms of a more significant problem. Jesus is the solution. God has chosen the local church, and His people deliver Christ to the world.

## SPIRITUAL ACTIVISM

Your church is the hope of your city. Its future is in jeopardy without a spiritual revival.

Today's church must rise to breathe life back into a dying world. The Gospel must be heard, disciples must be made, and spiritual activism is required.

*Webster's* dictionary defines activism as "a doctrine or practice that emphasizes direct vigorous action, especially in support of or opposition to one side of a controversial issue." Jesus commissioned us as spiritual activists when He gave us the mission to "make disciples of all nations'" (Matthew 28:19).

Jesus was history's most extraordinary activist. He knew His assignment, and He embraced it with unrelenting passion:

18 "The Spirit of the Lord is upon me, for he has anointed me to bring Good News to the poor. He has sent me to proclaim that captives will be released, that the blind will see, that the oppressed will be set free, 19 and that the time of the Lord's favor has come." (Luke 4:18-19)

Satan has set the world on fire. Only God's people and the local church carry the water capable of extinguishing the flames. To strengthen the church today and in the future, it must increase its commitment to reach and disciple a new generation for Christ. If your community is losing its grip on God, your church must act now to prevent secular or non-Christian influences from causing its spiritual destruction.

---

"The church represents the destination at which culture needs to and should arrive."
—Dr. Crawford Loritts

---

Local churches empowered by the Spirit and united in a common godly cause form an unbeatable force, leading to a world restored in Christ.

**KEEP IN MIND:**

1. The Church as a Lifeline: Local churches are the spiritual cornerstones of communities, essential for upholding their moral and spiritual health.

2. The Church's Resilience: The Church endures because its power lies not in buildings but in the hearts of its people.

3. Spiritual Activism is Crucial: To combat the rising secular and non-Christian trends, your church must engage in discipleship and spiritual activism to preserve and boost its impact.

Child trafficking and abuse threaten to destroy our youngest generations. Despite the efforts of governments and secular organizations, exploitation continues to grow. In the next chapter, we will uncover the root causes of child exploitation and demonstrate how the local church is uniquely positioned to be the world's most effective force against these atrocities.

## CHAPTER 4

# HOOK, LINE, AND ERADICATION: THE CHURCH'S ROLE IN ENDING CHILD TRAFFICKING

*"He has sent Me to heal the brokenhearted, to proclaim liberty to the captives and recovery of sight to the blind, to set at liberty those who are oppressed.*
—Luke 4:18

"The heart of the human problem is the problem of the human heart..."
—Billy Graham

It's not all fun and games.

Sarah Cooper was 15 when it started. Like millions of young girls on social media, she answers when a good-looking boy reaches out.

Sarah felt alienated and lonely. Her parents were unaware of her vulnerability. But she was a perfect candidate for those looking for 'her kind.' "I didn't want to listen to my mom, didn't want to listen to my dad," she claims.

Referring to herself as rebellious, Facebook became her way of finding a life of her own. "I was excited! Many people wanted to know me and wanted to be my friend! I had no idea who they were! Sometimes friend requests would come, and I would just add, add, add without even looking into it."

For over two years, Sarah communicated with her new online boyfriend. What began innocently advanced to where she started sharing explicit photos of herself.

Finally, the day came to meet.

"I didn't really know anything was wrong until I met him in person and saw his face; I finally realized he was closer to 40 than 18. Once I stepped into his car, it was too late. I was trafficked, given drugs, sold into sex slavery and held against my will at gunpoint. My instinct was to survive. I was lucky enough to have been rescued by a friend and thankfully survived my ordeal; some are not as lucky and never make it home."

Sarah now serves on the Survivors Council of ECPAT-USA, engaged in the fight against child trafficking worldwide.

Child trafficking continues to rise despite increased awareness, rescue, laws, and prosecutions. There is only one way to conquer this evil. It resides in the local church. This chapter will prove it to you. Read on.

## SEXTORTION (A MODERN FORM OF TRAFFICKING)

Emma was 16. Long black hair flowing over her tanned shoulders with a smile straight out of Heaven. She could have been a model.

Jacob was 15. Insecure. A little shy with girls. But in his heart, he prayed a girl like Emma would one day look his way.

It happened.

On a Wednesday night, at 11 p.m., Jacob was about to climb into bed. The sound from his computer shook him. "Bing!"

"Who is that?" he wondered. "I'll take a look."

It was not a typical friend request. Emma was the most beautiful girl he had ever seen. His heart pounded like Jamaican reggae drums! His mind raced: "Why does she want to meet ME? Was it a mistake?" But a message below her picture said, "Hi Jacob, My name is Emma. I noticed you on your profile. You are cute! Can we talk sometime?"

He couldn't hit the confirm button quickly enough! Jason did not sleep that night.

The morning sun shone through the blinds of his bedroom window at 6 am. He leaped from his bed square onto the seat of his computer chair. There it was: a new message.

It was her.

"Jason, this is Emma. How are you?"

After that quick introduction, a romance was born. At least, that is what Jason thought.

Daily chats became more personal. They had much in common. They were both from Indiana. They loved the same music. They laughed together as they shared stories about their families. They both loved but felt misunderstood by their parents.

Although they had yet to meet in person, neither seemed to care. Texting and chatting online was so great. Why change things?

After a few weeks, Jason asked himself, "Am I in love?"

Soon, Jason and Emma shared photos—Jason at a baseball game. Emma laughing with her friends at a coffee shop. Over time, the images became a bit more personal. Emma wearing her bikini at the beach. Jason strutting his physique in gym clothes.

Emma finally popped the question.

"Hey, Jason. Let's do something fun."

"Sure, he thought." Jason was game for anything. He wasn't about to risk disappointing the girl of his dreams.

"Jason, I'll send you a sexy picture of myself if you send me one first."

"What do you mean?"

"Just take off your clothes and stand in front of the mirror. Take a photo of yourself. Upload it to me. Once I get it, I'll do the same for you."

Jason could not get the fantasy image of her naked body out of his mind.

"Don't be nervous. It will be fun. And it will be our secret."

Jason hesitated. Something inside told him he shouldn't do it. But he was in too deep.

The next day, he hit the upload button.

Within an hour, Emma responded. "Wow. Nice body, Handsome! Now, here is what I want you to do. I want you to wire $3,000 to my bank account by Friday. If you don't, I will send your photo to every person on your contact list, including your parents. And, Jason, this is not a joke! I will do it."

White hot fear washed over his face. His throat went dry. He wanted to scream, but no sound was possible.

"$3,000?" Jason barely had $30 to his name.

Emma's real name was Angela. Angela lives in Manila, the Philippines, and works under the leadership of Maria Caparas, the international Queen of Sextortion. Dozens of girls share the office, sitting at computers, chatting with young teenage boys from the West, and grooming them to become blackmail victims like Jason.

For Angela, a girl born into poverty, it was the only job she could get. For Jason, it was more. It was the end.

"Mom and Dad, I'm so sorry to write this, but something terrible has happened to me. I can't explain it, but I hope you will forgive me. Tell Jessica I love her and to try hard at school. I love you, Jason."

Teen suicide, especially among boys, is escalating across America, making tragedies like Jason's death increasingly common.

The National Center for Missing or Exploited Children (NC-MEC) reports that in 2023, there were 26,718 reports of financial sextortion, up from 10,731 reports in 2022! Our children are under attack.[16]

## WHAT IS CHILD TRAFFICKING?

Trafficking is the leading, assisting, forcing, or coercing of a child to participate in sex, labor, or other activities that are immoral or illegal. It can include paying or enticing a child regardless of location, including within their own home. Paying children to participate in online sex, or exposing their bodies for the benefit of another person are also forms of trafficking. Abduction, fraud, deception, and the abuse of power by anyone, including parents, employers, teachers, or leaders, that end in maneuvering children for immoral or illegal acts are trafficking.

Human trafficking is a 150-billion-dollar industry.[17]

People have been enslaved since the beginning of recorded history. From conquered ancient civilizations to the kidnapping of children in the United States, children have worn the oppressive physical or emotional weights of bondage.

---

[16] MissingKids.org, NCMEC Releases New Sextortion Data;
https://www.missingkids.org/blog/2024/ncmec-releases-new-sextortion-data
[17] Ibid.

Child trafficking continues to rise, with about 7 million victims worldwide. Criminal organizations send 80 percent of these children into forced labor and 20 percent into the sex industry.

For traffickers, children are primary targets due to their trusting nature, inability to physically resist, and high profit potential.

Children from Burma are kidnapped to fishing boats or into shrimp factories in Thailand.

Children in India are stolen from busy train stations to haul bricks in small villages.

Local militias in the Democratic Republic of Congo kidnap children from local village families and transport them to rivers and caves. They dig for gold, diamonds, or the cobalt necessary for lithium-ion batteries for computers and electric vehicles.

Children in Mexico are kidnapped and held for ransom by cartels. Some run drugs. Others become soldiers. Still others are smuggled over the border into the United States for labor or sex.

## PEDERASTY: THE LOVE OF CHILDREN

Children have been exploited for thousands of years. The Greco-Roman world (800 years before Christ) provided philosophers such as Plato and Aristotle. Sex with children was an accepted lifestyle. They termed it pederasty, the love of children.

In Greece, men were driven by more than just lustful desires to commit this sin. They had societal and religious approval. Besides, Zeus permitted them.

Popular mythology written by Homer told a story that Zeus one day spotted a shepherd boy named Ganymede. The god either turned him into an eagle (or appointed an eagle) to carry Ganymede to Olympus. Zeus granted him immortality and the job of 'cupbearer of the gods.' This story was updated two centuries later, including Zeus taking Ganymede as his lover. It became the most common tale used to justify pederasty among wealthy Greek men.

Why should we be surprised? False gods determined the morality of Greek men.

Pederasty grew more prevalent and infiltrated the entire Roman world. Men's insatiable appetite for boys created a market for traffickers able to provide children for pedophiles. Jesus knew it. And it disgusted Him.[2] *"It would be better for them to be thrown into the sea with a millstone tied around their neck than to cause one of these little ones to stumble"* (Luke 17:2).

Without Jesus, the modern world might still be wondering if pedophilia and child sex trafficking are morally wrong.

However, despite Jesus' warnings in Luke, pedophilia continues today

Paul's companion Barnabas wrote his epistle between AD 70 and AD 132. The Christian author took a firm stand. "That we may avoid all injustice and impiety. We've been taught that to expose the newly born is the work of wicked men––first of all because we observe that almost all boys, as well as girls, are brought up for prostitution."

Satan attacks the young by presenting children as sex objects for spiritually damaged adults, including some self-proclaimed Christians.

Women who work on behalf of traffickers often visit poverty-stricken parents, offering money for their young children. They promise to pay for their education and provide jobs. Many mothers and fathers are unaware that traffickers quickly sell their children into forced labor or prostitution.

Worldwide, traffickers force 70 percent of trafficked girls into the commercial sex industry. Pedophiles' demand for boys is increasing.

The average age of children trafficked for sex ranges between 11 to 14.[18]

The U.S. Department of Health and Human Services estimates that between 240,000 and 325,000 children are at risk of sexual exploitation.[19]

## SEX TRAFFICKING AND THE INTERNET

In the United States, about 76 percent of sex transactions with underage girls begin on the internet[20]

Internet exploitation is on the rise. In the past, law enforcement relied on social media tips to apprehend traffickers. Those days are almost gone. The "dark net," a highly encrypted section of the internet, is a standard go-to place for child pornography and trafficking.

Social media platforms have transitioned to using encrypted messaging to preserve privacy. They claim internet crimes have decreased. However, this claim is disingenuous as nefarious activities now occur privately, invisible to law officials who might have been able to protect the child.

## ORGAN HARVESTING

In N'djamena, Chad (West Africa), over 30,000 children live on the streets. Criminals kidnap them to work in Cameroon or Nigeria as housekeepers or field workers. Others have their kidneys removed and sold to wealthy customers around the world. Organ harvesting is the fastest-growing segment of the trafficking industry. Kidnappers remove the child's healthy organs for sale in the marketplace. Many

---

[18] Monique Burr Foundation, Human Trafficking; https://mbfpreventioneducation.org/resource/human-trafficking/

[19] Assessing Risk of Commercial Sexual Exploitation Among Children Involved in the Child Welfare System, US Dept Health Human Services Sexual Exploitation, August 1, 2018.

[20] Ark of Hope, Trafficking of children; https://arkofhopeforchildren.org/table/issues/child-trafficking/

wealthy patients battling life-threatening illnesses are willing to spend highly on livers, kidneys, and hearts.

The World Health Organization (WHO) estimates that 10,000 kidneys are traded on the black market annually, more than one every hour! Kidneys from children as young as 6 years old can sell for over $150,000. Organ vendors are active in North and West Africa, China, Israel, Pakistan, Egypt, Haiti, and even the United States.

A teenage girl from Egypt was rushed to a hospital in Cairo for an appendectomy. While unconscious, the doctor removed her kidney as well. She was unaware of it for years. After moving to Canada, she visited her doctor for a routine medical check-up.

"When did you have your kidney removed?" asked the doctor.

"I didn't," she replied.

"You did."

Organ harvesting returns about 1.7 billion dollars to the world economy. Roughly 10 percent of transplants are illegal.[21] Many of those organs are from vulnerable children.

## ARE YOUR CHILDREN AT RISK?

Most parents choose to believe their children are safe. Mothers and fathers are more diligent than ever in teaching their children how to respond to strangers, even those who seem friendly.

So why are many of these children willing to walk away with someone they just met?

## TRAFFICKING: THE AFTER-SCHOOL TECHNIQUE

Around the world, traffickers patrol near schools, seeking a solitary child waiting for their ride home. The friendly trafficker (often a woman) will walk up to the child. Here is a typical conversation:

---

[21] The Exodus Road, Exodus Road Organ Trafficking Facts

"Hello, Honey. What is your name?"

"I'm Mary."

"Hi Mary. Who are you waiting for?"

"My Mom."

"What is your mother's name?"

"Linda."

"Yes! I am a friend of your mother, Linda. She is not feeling well and asked me to pick you up from school."

Children are prone to trust friendly women. Hand in hand, the child willingly climbs into the trafficker's car.

## THE PUPPY DOG TECHNIQUE

The head of an anti-trafficking organization recently collaborated with local police on the following experiment: They entered a park where several children were playing. The leader introduced himself to a young mother sitting on a bench and said: "I will bet you I will convince your child to walk away with me in 30 seconds."

"Impossible!" she exclaimed. My husband and I have often spoken to him about 'stranger danger.' We have role-played with him and reminded him regularly. He would never walk away with a stranger!"

With the police nearby, she agreed to the test.

The founder strolled up to the 5-year-old child. Smiling, he held an adorable six-week-old puppy. The little boy's eyes widened, and giggled as he stroked the puppy's downy face.

"You know, my puppy has some brothers and sisters. They miss him. They are just as cute as he is. They would love to meet you. Would you like to go see them?"

"Yes! Please!" the boy shouted!

The mother watched in horror as her son cheerfully slipped his hand into the stranger's grasp and skipped away.

It's all about trust.

Little children equate kindness with safety. From a child's perspective, they cannot understand why a kind person would be dangerous. Traffickers understand children's sensitive natures. They share their knowledge. They constantly add new techniques to stay one step ahead of the law. But there is one common denominator: kindness. It is the bridge to exploitation.

## FOUR COMMON SOLUTIONS

There are four widespread responses to trafficking: Awareness, Rescue, Recovery, and Prosecution.

## AWARENESS

Awareness campaigns are the most common. Movies, documentaries, government agencies, churches, and nonprofit organizations educate and warn parents, caregivers, school teachers, and daycare workers about the dangers of child trafficking.

Awareness strategies are essential and have helped to provide a shield against victimization.

However, besides warning the 'good guys', they also inspire the bad ones. These campaigns highlight the appeal and profitability of child trafficking to those with malicious intentions. Each year, more traffickers enter the industry than are apprehended.

## RESCUE

Each day, people risk their lives to rescue children from the criminal enterprise of trafficking.

*"Rescue the weak and the needy; deliver them from the hand of the wicked"* (Psalm 82:4).

Yet, rescue efforts fall short. For every child saved, many more enter slavery.

Pattaya, Thailand, is one of the most common destinations for children trafficked into the sex industry. Pedophiles especially seek children under 12 years old. They are often placed in basement rooms beneath nightclubs and taught to perform specific acts. When they reach an age where they can be styled to look like 18-year-olds, they receive training to perform on nightclub stages or are sent out onto the streets for prostitution. Girls dance on stage to entice men, leaving with them for an hour or less. Some popular girls have up to 20 'dates' a night.

Why don't these girls leave the industry? They and their families are often threatened. Perhaps even more significantly, most girls and boys are trafficked into nightclubs when they are between 10 and 15 years old. They establish friendships with other trafficked victims. They lean on one another for support and love. They become so bonded they are unwilling to leave.

Although some are rescued, most return despite the horrific living conditions and the physical or emotional abuse at the hands of the traffickers. Since they have little or no education, they feel ill-equipped to re-enter public school. A rescued girl is often found talking on her phone with trafficked friends, who attempt to persuade her to 'return home.' She often will.

## RECOVERY

Rescued victims suffer from a myriad of physical ailments due to poor nutrition, torture, or psychological abuse. They often struggle with post-traumatic stress disorder or a host of other emotional issues. Many are spiritually damaged, doubting the existence of a God who would allow them to suffer at the hands of criminals.

Physical, psychological, and spiritual healing takes time, expertise, and funding. Low financial resources and undertrained personnel limit the recovery efforts. Orphanages and rescue centers are filled with rescued children but lack enough qualified medical and spiritual professionals to restore them to health.

It is essential to provide formal education for emotionally wounded children. Yet returning to school is often impossible. Having missed several school years, they are older than their classmates and frequently mocked. They have little confidence to perform well.

Vocational training is often a successful strategy to help children return to society. Many excellent Christian organizations help rescued girls and boys learn marketable trades such as barbering, sewing, etc. They live together to form new peer groups, encouraging each other to stay strong. They learn to love one another as they struggle to separate themselves from their past. And they learn to embrace Jesus as Friend and Savior. Children find healing, recovery, and hope.

Many of these organizations thrive and empower victims around the world. Yet most are expensive to operate and understaffed without enough trained teachers.

## PROSECUTION

There are more anti-trafficking laws and prosecution attempts than ever. Yet these efforts are often thwarted. Criminal organizations can easily hire top-level attorneys or bribe officials and politicians to stay in business.

The secular world does its best to reduce the menace of child trafficking. Yet it continues to increase. Awareness, Rescue, Recovery, and Prosecution cannot rescue, recover, and prosecute with enough effectiveness or speed to overtake the number of children victimized each year.

Is there nothing we can do?

The prophet Habakkuk felt that way. He believed God would fix the problem. Finally, he hit the wall: He had witnessed too much death and destruction, and he let God have it!

*[2]"How long, O Lord, must I call for help? But you do not listen! 'Violence is everywhere!' I cry, but you do not come to save.[3] Must I forever see these evil deeds? Why must I watch all this misery?"* —Habakkuk 1:2-4.

## THE BEST SHORT-TERM SOLUTION: PREVENTION

Awareness, Rescue, Recovery, and Prosecution are essential strategies to combat the scourge of trafficking. However, one approach is most successful: Prevention.

Social media is the most common and impactful tool traffickers and exploiters use today. It is their way of breaking into the vulnerable souls of your children. The parents (and church) are responsible for protecting them while they are still young. Act now!

As a parent, your Biblical role is to protect your child.

*"Speak up for those who cannot speak for themselves; ensure justice for those being crushed."* (Proverbs 31:8)

Children between the ages of 10 and 16 are especially vulnerable. As they transition from childhood to adulthood, they strive for independence while experiencing self-doubts. They look to friends and others for approval and encouragement. They can visualize having an attractive boyfriend or girlfriend but doubt their own attractiveness. In short, they are insecure.

Not all kids are this way. Yet, most are. Christian children are no different. It's a natural part of growing up. But it's also what makes them vulnerable to exploitation, primarily online.

Social media surrounds a child's life. Facebook, TikTok, Instagram, YouTube, Snapchat and Twitter (X) are well known. Yet additional platforms have entered the fray. BeReal, Roblox, Spotify, Twitch, or Gas all offer opportunities to meet strangers online.

Nearly all children today own a smartphone. Children replace outdoor play with online play. Young people choose online relationships rather than real ones. Childhood depression, self-harm, and suicide rates continue to climb.

Prying eyes intercept chat messages, searching for opportunities to strike. They watch as kids share their worries, traumas, or complaints. At the opportune time, one of them receives a new friend request, and the grooming begins.

Dr. Jonathan Haidt, in his best-selling book The Anxious Generation, suggests that parents take the lead in the following areas:

1. Expand opportunities for children to play outside with mixed-aged groups and limited adult supervision (Allowing children to initiate and build relationships without the feeling of 'prying eyes').

2. Be intentional in finding ways to engage children in what he terms 'real-world communities,' (rather than false online ones).

3. Let your child's first phone be designed only for communication (rather than a smartphone).

4. Wait until high school to give children their first smartphone. (He suggests gathering other parents to commit the same.)

With this strategy, can you be assured that kids will not occasionally use a friend's smartphone? Of course not. But the risk of becoming a victim is significantly reduced if your child is not the smartphone owner.

What can you do to make computers safer for your kids? This is when it is time to toughen up: Install 'parental control' filters on your children's computers! They'll almost certainly complain. They may even become angry (hint: You may need to remind them who is in charge). Don't become the parent who compromises your child's safety for popularity. They'll forgive you (eventually).

As a church leader, take a stand to safeguard children from online exploitation and recruit parents to lead in this effort. Assign a leader to form a child protection group, seeking strategies and tools to assist church-going parents in their efforts to protect their children.

## THE ULTIMATE SOLUTION: JESUS AND THE CHURCH

Awareness, Rescue, Recovery, and Prosecution strategies are helpful. Prevention strategies are essential. But like a weed, trafficking will keep returning unless we eliminate the root cause.

Jesus nailed it.

[19] *"For out of the heart come evil thoughts—murder, adultery, sexual immorality, theft, false testimony, slander"* (Matthew 15:19).

Traffickers have no inner voice strong enough to combat their desire for wealth, power, and lust. Sin's influence upon them is as irresistible as the pull of Earth's magnetic north is to a compass. Without a superior force to overcome its power, traffickers inevitably yield.

[17] *"The sinful nature wants to do evil, which is just the opposite of what the Spirit wants. And the Spirit gives us desires that are the opposite of what the sinful nature desires. These two forces are constantly fighting each other, so you are not free to carry out your good intentions"* (Galatians 5:17 NLT).

It begins from conception. In the womb, our mother meets all our needs. It's a good life, at least for about nine months. Once we are born, we naturally expect the same treatment. And if our mother fails to meet expectations, we cry and throw tantrums. If that process continues indefinitely, we become entitled. We may even continue the tantrums. Perhaps that is a bit simplistic. But you get the point.

Our self-centeredness can manufacture the evil thoughts referred to by Jesus (Matthew 15:19). The more we dwell on these thoughts, the more comfortable they become. They gain power until we begin to feel entitled to act upon them. And they are destructive.

*15 "Then, after desire has conceived, it gives birth to sin; and sin, when it is full-grown, gives birth to death"* (James 1:15).

That is where you come in.

The best way to combat trafficking is to cultivate a new generation of Jesus-centered adults who do not harbor the evil thoughts that lead to this sin. And, for the few who might, they will possess the spiritual power to overcome those thoughts. Who is this generation we speak of?

They are the children of today.

Since trafficking is a spiritual problem, spiritual solutions are required.

## THE CHURCH

God is calling the church and His people to find and raise a new generation who will not participate in trafficking, for they will not harbor the thoughts leading to the actions.

Children are the most receptive to embrace Jesus and the values He teaches. In a few short years they will enter the adult world. And, if you do your job, they will change it.

*8 "They would not be like their ancestors—a stubborn and rebellious generation, whose hearts were not loyal to God, whose spirits were not faithful to him."* (Psalms 78:8)

Ending exploitation is not an overnight exercise. But unless we address the spiritual root cause, it will continue to steal our children and our future generations. Will it disappear before Jesus comes again? Not entirely. But we can impede its momentum and begin to reclaim the ones Satan has targeted for attack.

When Jesus arrives, He will finish the job.

What can you do today? For the short term, support the efforts of Awareness, Rescue, Recovery, and Prosecution. Participate in Prevention strategies.

Never take your foot off the gas to rescue victims, offer vocational care, build awareness, and prosecute those who harm children. Participate in prevention strategies for the internet and social media. Create opportunities for children to build genuine relationships above those formed online.

Rather than treating only the symptom, it is up to the church to treat the disease. Trafficking is a sickness. The only vaccine is Jesus.

Strengthen your commitment to reach and disciple today's children, the next generation of adults for Christ. Imprint God's morals on their hearts. Cultivate in them a desire for God that surpasses their attraction to sin. Teach them scriptures that command them to protect the weak[22] and defend the oppressed.[23] Empower them with the indestructible armor of God.[24] In the battle against trafficking, only Christ can prevail. It's time to take up arms.

## KEEP IN MIND:

1. Prevention is The Most Effective Strategy: Awareness, rescue, and rehabilitation remain essential, but prevention is the most potent weapon to protect children from exploitation.

---

[22] Pslams 8:3; ³"Defend the weak and the fatherless; uphold the cause of the poor and the oppressed."

[23] Isaiah 1:17; "Learn to do right; seek justice. Defend the oppressed.[a] Take up the cause of the fatherless; plead the case of the widow."

[24] Ephesians 6:10; ¹⁰"Finally, be strong in the Lord and in his mighty power."

2. Spiritual Solutions are Essential: Child exploitation stems from sinful hearts. Eradication requires raising children for Christ, creating a new generation of adults who reshape communities to reflect Godly values.

3. The Church Must Take the Lead: Local churches should train and encourage parents to prohibit smartphones for their youngest children, and add anti-trafficking filters to computers.

Shores are still cluttered with ancient ships, lost to hurricanes, storms, and towering waves centuries ago. Better preparation before departure could have prevented many of these tragedies. The next chapter will outline essential steps to prepare your ship for a successful and safe voyage.

## CHAPTER 5

# CHARTING A CLEAR COURSE: CHURCH VISION, ASSESSMENT, AND GOALS

*"Or suppose a king is about to go to war against another king. Won't he first sit down and consider whether he is able with ten thousand men to oppose the one coming against him with twenty thousand?"*
—Luke 14:31

"If you fail to plan, you are planning to fail."
—Benjamin Franklin

Vision is not a verb.

It was August 28, 1963. Baptist minister Dr. Martin Luther King Jr stood to address over 200,000 people gathered in Washington, D.C. He stood at the foot of the Lincoln Memorial and read his most famous and quoted speech. King's "I Had a Dream" speech became a force so powerful that thousands of people memorized it in full. It created a powerful and captivating image in the hearts of people from every ethnicity, accelerating the advancement of civil rights. King's speech was a vision of the future, a world reborn in the image of God, His people walking together in unity and love, despite their differences.

*"I have a dream....one day right down in Alabama little black boys and black girls will be able to join hands with little white boys and white girls as sisters and brothers."*

Martin Luther King's dream drove people of all colors to develop plans that would work toward racial reconciliation. His vision created a mental picture that people could strive toward. A contractor sees his building's completion even before creating the blueprint. An artist sees the picture before he picks up the brush. Students imagine walking across the stage at their graduation ceremony before entering college. A pastor imagines a vibrant, growing church before he outlines a plan to achieve it.

## JASON'S VISION

Jason had a dream. He visualized it for three years: His first car. It didn't need to be new. It just needed to be cool. Red would work. Perhaps blue. No dents. Something that high school girls might like. He was 16 and he felt it was time. All he needed to do was convince Dad.

Jason's father was the pastor of a local church. Although he was fair minded, his son knew it would be a difficult conversation. His dad never missed an opportunity to remind him that grace is the one thing that comes without a price tag; everything else must be earned.

Jason knocked on his father's office door. "Come on in, son!" Looking at his dad sitting behind his large maple desk, he stammered out his first words. "Dad, I've been dreaming of a car since I was 13. I just got my driver's license. And I know you offered me your second-hand station wagon to drive to school, but really, Dad...a station wagon? I'd rather take the bus than be the laughingstock of the entire school!"

His father, immersed in writing his weekly sermon, looked up. He feigned surprise but was impressed with his son's boldness. "Indeed," he thought. "He is becoming a man."

"Tell me what you want, son."

"I want a car that I can show off to my friends, something I'm not embarrassed to drive. It doesn't have to be new, Dad. But it has to look cool!"

As his father pondered a response, his mouth revealed a small smile. An idea had landed.

"I'll tell you what son. Christmas is four months away. I'll give you an assignment. If you complete it, you will get your car...and we can ensure it is cool!"

Jason nearly flipped! There was no price he would not be willing to pay!

"Son, there are 3 things I want you to do. If you do them by December 15th, I will purchase your car for Christmas."

Jason's imagination ran wild. He could almost feel his hand upon the steering wheel. He envisioned the red (perhaps blue) glossy exterior. He imagined the soft thud of the car door closing as he sat in the leather (perhaps vinyl) driver's seat. He subconsciously smelled the imitation wood grain dashboard. Imaginary music from his future car stereo filled his mind, making him move to beats that weren't yet playing.

"Anything, Dad! I'll do it!"

"Ok, first I want you to get at least a B in every subject this quarter."

"No problem, Dad!"

"Next, I want you to read at least one chapter of the Bible each night. And, Jason, your mother will be checking on this."

"Consider it done, Dad!"

"Finally, I've been looking at your hair. It has been hanging to the middle of your back for over a year. I know you like it. But I want you to cut it to at least shoulder length."

"Dad, I'll do it!"

Time passed. On December 15, Jason knocked on his father's office door.

"Dad, I'm excited to talk about getting my car!"

"Well, Jason, you did well. I just looked at your school grades and saw that you achieved straight A's in your classes! Well done! Also, your mother told me yesterday that you have immersed yourself in Bible study, sometimes reading 2 or 3 chapters each night. I'm very proud of you!!!" His father paused, and then began slowly, "But, son, one thing is holding up this project. You still have not cut your hair!"

Jason, in many ways, was like his father, well prepared. He was ready for the challenge and had prepared an answer he knew his dad couldn't counter. "Dad, I knew you would ask me about that. I was considering cutting my hair, but when reading the Bible, I read about Moses. And, from what I understand, he had long hair! So I continued to read further and discovered the story of Samson. Imagine my surprise to learn he also had long hair! In fact, it was his long hair that gave him his strength! And, I have to point this out, Dad. I've been looking at that photo on the wall directly behind you. Every time I come into your office I see it hanging there. It is a picture of our Lord Jesus. And, Dad, do you know what? He looks great in his long hair! So, here is what I've concluded; If long hair was good enough for Moses, Samson, and Jesus I think it is only reasonable that it is good enough for me! So, Dad, how about getting me that car?"

His father was, again, impressed. But he was not a fool. "Son, you are correct. Moses, as far as we know, had long hair. And, yes, there is no debate that Sampson also had long hair. And indeed, whenever I think of our Lord Jesus, I also imagine him with long hair."

Jason smiled. He knew that he not only convinced his father. He knew he would soon be driving the car of his dreams!

"But Jason, do you know what else they had in common?"

Jason had a feeling that Dad was about to, again, pull out some unexpected wisdom.

"They WALKED everywhere they went!"

The next day was predictable. Dad and Jason shopped for a 'cool' car. Dad in his blue jeans and long-sleeved plaid shirt; Jason with a fresh new haircut.

Jason dreamed of it. Then he did what was necessary to achieve it.

## A VISION 'ROCKED' PETER'S WORLD

Anointed as the 'rock of the church' Peter was highly motivated. His vision was a transformed Jewish community. Like most of us, Peter soon realized his vision was too small (Acts 10:9-16). Through the power of a dream, Peter was exposed to a Gospel with no racial limits, surpassing the Jewish community to reach the Gentiles—an unexpected vision; a shocking one for a person so immersed in the Jewish culture. God commanded Peter to reach a wider audience, to push past his comfort zone. But there was an upside: He was allowed to expand his diet (His mind was suddenly flooded with mouthwatering images of barbecued pork ribs).

God's vision propelled Peter into action. He popped downstairs to find three men to take him to Cornelius, a Gentile "God-fearing" Roman Centurion. Peter (still likely in shock) found himself preaching Christ to Cornelius's Gentile friends.

## VISION

A vision is a mental image that depicts the future. It is emotional, magnetic, colorful, and motivating. It motivates you to make decisions that increase your chances of success. If it is meaningful enough you will fight for it.

Paul's vision was just like that. *[14] "I press on to reach the end of the race and receive the heavenly prize for which God, through Christ Jesus, is calling us"* (Phil 3:14 NLT).

For Paul, the prize was worth the price!

Jesus presented a vision that inspired Jesus' followers to tolerate even the harshest treatment for the sake of Heaven.

*[11] "Blessed are you when people insult you, persecute you and falsely say all kinds of evil against you because of me. [12] Rejoice and be glad, because great is your reward in heaven..."* (Matthew 5:11-12)

## ASSESS OR REGRESS

*"...Don't think you are better than you really are. Be honest in your evaluation of yourselves, measuring yourselves by the faith God has given us."* (Romans 12:3)

As a young man I found myself deep in debt. I didn't want to be. But it seemed that every bank in America believed I was a valuable and trustworthy person. Every few weeks another credit card showed up in the mail with my name nicely embossed. All I had to do was call a toll-free number and I would have money to spend! It sounded too good to be true...It was. It did not take long before realizing that these seemingly generous banks were not so generous after all. They wanted their money back, with interest.

Cleverly, they left me an out-clause. If I would agree to pay the minimum amount each month, I could simply roll over the balance for the future. As a not-so-savvy 22-year-old it felt like a miracle! I had yet to learn about the miracle of compounding interest rates.

It got worse. Sinking slowly down a rabbit hole of financial devastation, I visited a friend looking for sympathy to join me in my anger toward the banks. I spoke. I yelled. I complained for hours. Finally he responded.

"Gary, you are exactly where you have chosen to be." I almost hit him. Are you kidding?? Who would choose being buried in debt and eating canned corn as my daily meal?

Sometimes the hard truth is what is needed. In this case, my friend's words were wise so I made an assessment; I realized that my situation was due entirely to the choices I made along the way. Instead of blaming the banks, I got busy. I compared where I was to where I wanted to be. I developed a fresh strategy and made new choices.

It took discipline, but mostly a new mentality. I remember writing the check to pay off my final debt. I was free. I was free indeed.

If your ministry is not where you want it to be, look in the mirror. Even if someone else is to blame, it's a waste of time to do it. Assess where you are and determine to make new choices, even if they are beyond your comfort zone. It will be worth it.

Take the time to be thorough, and assess your situation honestly. Compare it to your vision. Measure the gap between your current situation and where you want to be.

[28] *"Suppose one of you wants to build a tower. Won't you first sit down and estimate the cost to see if you have enough money to complete it?* (Luke 14:28).

"You can't get where you are going if you don't know where you are." (anonymous).

## GAP ASSESSMENT TABLE

To reach your vision, it is helpful first to quantify it in measurable numbers. Then you can measure the distance you have to go. It is essential to quantify numbers. Do not be vague. Know precisely what will define success for your church or ministry.

The table below is an example, but you should make one that fits your church perfectly. Update it monthly. Post it on your wall for all to see. Look at it daily. Let it constantly remind you where you are and how you are progressing.

| | Church Attendance (min 2 X per month) | | Evangelism (Salvation Prayers/ month) | | Discipleship (Formal curriculum) | |
|---|---|---|---|---|---|---|
| | 5 Yr Vision | Current Number | 5 Yr Vision | Current Number | 5 Yr Vision | Current Number |
| Children (Pre-school) | 20 | | 5 | | 4 | |
| Children (Age 5-12) | 25 | | 8 | | 6 | |
| Youth (Middle School) | 25 | | 8 | | 6 | |
| Youth (High School) | 30 | | 6 | | 5 | |
| Young Adults (18-22) | 30 | | 5 | | 4 | |
| Young Adults (23-29) | 35 | | 4 | | 3 | |
| Adults (30-49) | 40 | | 3 | | 2 | |
| Adults (50-69) | 40 | | 2 | | 2 | |
| Adults (70-79) | 20 | | 1 | | 1 | |
| Adults (80+) | 10 | | 1 | | 1 | |

Now is the time to get some courage. Share your vision and Gap Assessment with your leaders and congregation. Let them see the quantifiable gap between today and what will define success. Let them know of your commitment and ask for their participation.

Congregations, like good soldiers, need mission clarity. That is your responsibility. If you make them part of your team, they will pray, volunteer, and seek opportunities to help your vision become reality. Your role is to paint a clear vision, quantify success, set achievable goals and keep that vision alive!

## GOALS: GOD'S ROADMAP TO YOUR DESTINATION

*"...Whoever walks in the dark does not know*
*where they are going."*
—John 12:35

Perfection of means and confusion of goals seem, in my
opinion, to characterize our age.
—Albert Einstein

Recently, a group of children were questioned about their life goals.

"What are your life goals?" (to a 10-year-old boy)

1. "Get a girlfriend"
2. "Kiss her"
3. "Rule the world" (This may have been mine)

A 5-year-old boy responded:

"Someday I will have so much food to eat that I will explode!" (Stand clear)

Finally, this one:

"What is your vision for when you grow up?"

"To be like Lebron James and play in the NBA."

"What do you need to accomplish your goal?"

1. "Get bigger."
2. "Shave my head."
3. "Be black."

Kids are great. They are dreamers. They are not afraid of vision. And, like the Lebron James wannabes, they embrace step-by-step plans.

14 *"I press on toward the goal to win the prize for which God has called me heavenward in Christ Jesus"* (Phil 3:12-14).

Few Bible colleges or seminaries teach goal setting. Perhaps it seems too secular to them. It is not.

## WHAT IS YOUR COOKIE?

When I was a kid, we always knew what we were having for Sunday dinner. Mom shopped for groceries on Fridays. Each excursion included a stroll down the canned food aisle. Mom was always looking for something exotic, not wanting to have bored kids. Had she asked, I would have been content with cookies and licorice as my staple diet.

Nearly each Friday, she would stop halfway down aisle 6, look to the right, and spot the worst food known to humankind: Chung King Chow Mein.

Chung King brand was (gratefully) removed from society in the late 90's. I can now share my feelings without fear of a lawsuit. Chung King Chow Mein consisted of two cans, one wrapped atop the other. Hard brown dry noodles filled the top. They threatened to break your rear molars with every bite. Inside the bottom can was a pasty goo. Bathing in that solution were sliced water chestnuts, celery pieces and what seemed to be something slightly like chicken. It was, by my account, the undisputed scourge of the universe. Created by the Devil with the intent of traumatizing children and wrecking their health, he convinced American mothers that their kids loved the stuff. Luckily we survived. That's when I knew God was real.

This weekly experience destroyed not only my appetite for Chinese food. It ruined my interest in China. That is, until that day when we were driving down the road and spotted a little Chinese Restaurant on Evergreen Way. Mom pulled in. Terror filled the backseat where my brother, sister, and I were sitting. We were convinced the restaurant was simply shopping at the same store as Mom. Out of sight, they would huddle on the kitchen floor, pry open the can, snicker quietly at their devious crime, pour it into a large bowl and bring it out to our table. Chung King!

Mom convinced us that the restaurant would supply a fortune cookie for each customer if we finished our dinner.

That was motivation enough for me. I loved fortune cookies. They were sweet, and they always had good news.

The story ends well. The Chinese food was passable. We continued to eat at the restaurant monthly. We tolerated their chow mein. But make no mistake about it. I came for the cookie.

Everything begins with a vision (the cookie). Yet it is merely a dream without a plan (eating the dinner). A plan is only a hope if it lacks the specific steps to guide you forward (the individual bites). Goals are the bites, the steps, you take as you journey forward toward your vision.

## GOALS (BIBLICALLY SPEAKING)

2 *"Then the Lord replied: "Write down the revelation and make it plain on tablets."* (Habakkuk 2:2)

Goals are road markers. Put them in order, in a straight line toward your vision and you have it. Simple. Most people do not do them. Even less write them down.

Psychology Professor Dr. Gail Matthews, a clinical psychologist from Dominican University of California led a study in 2005. She separated participants into five groups, each with different instructions.

Group One was given unwritten goals. Group Two wrote their goals down. Group Three wrote both goals and their commitments to action. Group Four wrote their goals, action commitments, and shared them with a friend. And Group Five passed their written goals, action commitments, and weekly updates to a friend.

Of the participants who wrote down their goals, actions and provided weekly progress to a friend, 76 percent successfully achieved their goals, far higher than any other group! Multiple additional studies from universities have conducted similar projects with similar results. Successful businesses require employees to write and review goals. Churches and ministries around the world do the same. Do it.

## SMART VS SMARTER GOALS

Many organizations train their leaders to use the acronym SMART when setting goals. The letters represent Specific, Measurable, Achievable, Relevant, and Time-Bound. Although these are simple and effective steps, they are insufficient for today's Christian world.

I often conduct a "Biblically Based Goal Setting" workshop in several nations. I've discovered that although most pastors have extensive education in theology and church administration they are under-trained in effective goal-setting.

A Godly vision without a written plan is a dream. A plan without God-guided goals is rarely effective.

[9] "*A man's heart plans his way, But the Lord directs his steps*" (Proverbs 16:9).

One of the limitations in the business version of goal setting is the insinuation that we can fully control outcomes. This wrong idea can tempt people to manipulate others to achieve personal goals. Occasionally this happens in the sales world.

An unscrupulous life-insurance salesperson may set a goal to sell a policy by Friday. As the day approaches, he realizes he has yet to sell one. Committed to his goal he meets a married couple and presents them a policy. Although they request time to consider the offer, he impatiently manipulates them into an immediate sale, accomplishing his goal.

Christian ministry is different. Biblical goal setting does not require manipulation. Goals are based on our actions rather than other people's responses to them.

For ministry purposes, I've edited the business acronym of SMART to another I call SMARTER.

S—-Specific and Stretching. Goals must be precise, easy to understand, and challenge you to stretch. Easy-to-reach goals do not result in growth.

M—-Measurable. Goals should be measurable for regular tracking and assessment.

A—-Agreed Upon. Every member of your team must buy-into your vision, plan, and goals. One disagreeing teammate can bring negativity that cripples your entire project.

R—-Realistic. Although goals must require you to stretch, they must be achievable. Teams will become discouraged with failure and lose their motivation. Make goals "just out of reach but not out of sight." (Dennis Waitley)

T—-Time Based. Goals must have a written deadline for completion. And you, as a leader, need to remind people of that deadline before it arrives.

E—-Exciting. People are driven by collective vision and emotion. Envision the achievement of the team goal and describe it enthusiastically to your team. Your excitement and conviction are crucial to inspire others to share your feelings!

R—-Recorded and Reviewed. Goals must be written down and reviewed regularly! It does little good to write them effectively and then file into a black hole! Print them and put them on your desk where you see them regularly. Out of sight means out of mind!

Written and reviewed goals act as a mission-focused GPS, continuously adjusting your path toward your destination.

### Keep in Mind:

1. Vision Drives Action: A compelling vision is a mental picture of the accomplished mission. It inspires and directs strategic decisions, driving team members toward achieving meaningful goals.

2. Honest Assessment is Essential: Regularly perform an honest assessment of the gap between your current ministry situation and your vision.

3. SMARTER Goals Lead to Success: Clear, challenging, and frequently reviewed goals keep the church on track and moving toward its vision with God's help.

Watch out for underwater obstacles that might spring a leak in your boat as you set sail with your goals. In the next chapter we will look at some of them and what you can do to keep your ship afloat!

## CHAPTER 6

# UNDERWATER OBSTACLES: BARRIERS THAT CAN SINK YOUR SHIP

[8] *"For my thoughts are not your thoughts, neither are your ways my ways," declares the Lord."*
—Isaiah 55:8

"Old ways of doing things cease to be effective, though they may have been very powerful in the past. There arises a very real danger that we will set ourselves in opposition to what God truly is doing now and aims to do in the future."
— Dallas Willard, *Renovation of the Heart: Putting on the Character of Christ*

M any ship captains have regretted overlooking the hidden reefs beneath the water's surface. In this chapter, we will discuss three things that can stop your church in its tracks: Traditions, outdated paradigms, and the unwillingness to pivot.

## THE TRADITION TRAP

A Seattle church introduced its new pastor to the congregation. When the Lord's prayer was recited, he was surprised to see half the congregants stand up while the rest remained in their seats.

The seated ones began yelling for the others to sit down. The standing ones yelled for the seated ones to stand up!

The new pastor became frustrated, not knowing the church tradition. After service, his staff suggested he call a 98-year-old man, one of the church's founders.

"Pastor," he asked, "Is the tradition to stand during this prayer?"

The old man answered, "No, that is not the tradition."

The new pastor was relieved. "Then the tradition is to sit!" he proclaimed!

The old man answered, "No, that is not the tradition."

The confused young pastor told the old man, "But the congregants fight all the time, yelling at each other about whether they should sit or stand."

The old pastor interrupted, exclaiming, "Yes! *THAT* is the tradition!"

*You have let go of the commands of God and are holding on to human traditions"* (Mark 7:8).

## WHAT'S HE DOING ON THE ROOF?

One of my favorite movies is "Fiddler on the Roof."

Tevye is a milkman in the small Russian Jewish village of Anatevka. As the movie begins, he turns to the camera, explaining to the audience that ancient traditions were the glue holding the community together. Traditions bound the people of Anatevka to one another and God.

Tevye explains: "Because of our traditions, we've kept our balance for many years. Here in Anatevka we have traditions for everything: how to sleep, how to eat, how to work, how to wear clothes. For instance, we always keep our heads covered and wear a little prayer shawl. This shows our constant devotion to God.

You may ask, how did this tradition get started? I'll tell you how—I don't know!"

## WHERE'S THE BEEF?

A young married couple would take turns cooking meals for one another. But both looked forward to those special times when the wife would cook a succulent roast beef. After a year of marriage, the young husband asked his bride "Honey, I notice that every time you prepare to cook, you cut off the ends of the beef and throw them away. I'm not complaining. It always tastes great. But why do you do that?"

He was expecting a culinary answer. But she surprised him.

"I learned it from my mother. She always cuts off the ends of the beef before cooking."

A few weeks later, the couple were visiting the wife's family. He couldn't help but ask his mother-in-law. "Each time your daughter makes roast beef, she cuts off the ends of the meat and throws it away. She said she learned it from you. Why do you do that?"

"Honey," she said, "I learned it from my mother."

Finally, the entire family gathered during the Christmas season. As luck had it, his wife's grandmother was there. "Gran," the young husband said, "My wife always cuts off the ends of the roast beef before she cooks it. She learned it from your daughter. And your daughter said she learned it from you. Why do you do it?"

She looked at him with surprise. "It's simple. My roasting pan is only six inches long!"

What about church customs? What seems normal, did not begin that way.

When exactly did we decide that church should begin with 20 minutes of worship, followed by 5 minutes of announcements and 30 minutes of sermon?

Why do we sit in rows instead of tables? Why do we preach to a silent group instead of engaging them with discussion?

---

"The important thing is not to stop questioning."
—Albert Einstein

---

I'm NOT suggesting you change your church format. But are you willing to change some of your traditions to keep them relevant for today? Have some of them become so ingrained that there is a gap between them and your ever-changing community?

Stephen Covey's book *Trust and Inspire* encourages organizations to "collaborate and innovate successfully enough to stay highly relevant in a changing, disruptive world."

Microsoft CEO Satya Nadella states, "Our industry respects innovation, not tradition."

Innovation is the result of remaining relevant in a fluctuating world. If we cannot achieve this goal, the gap between the church and community will continue to widen.

## WHAT YOU HOLD CAN BEGIN TO MOLD

Assess your deeply embedded methods. Are they still relevant? Don't be afraid to experiment. Many churches update their worship styles to stay in tune with current music trends, but consider other changes non-negotiable. What are your non-negotiables?

Get past the fear of change. Take some chances. Take some advice from the great Will Rogers who proclaimed, "Even if you are on the right track, you'll get run over if you just sit there."

Traditions help define us. They link us to the past. But be careful they do not prevent you from reaching your full potential.

## DOES YOUR PARADIGM NEED A SHIFT?

It's not what you look at that matters, it's what you see.
—Henry David Thoreau

In the ever-evolving quest to make simple things more complicated, Merriam-Webster's dictionary defined paradigm this way:

Paradigm: a philosophical and theoretical framework of a scientific school or discipline within which theories, laws, and generalizations and the experiments performed in support of them are formulated (such as the Freudian paradigm of psychoanalysis).

Or in other words, 'the way we see stuff.'

Brad Paisley's country song, "I'm Still a Guy," shared the difference between how he and his wife viewed a beautiful young deer.

"When you see a deer, you see Bambi,
And I see antlers up on the wall"

What seems natural to us is often seen as evil by God.

"...The Lord does not look at the things people look at. People look at the outward appearance, but the Lord looks at the heart" (1 Samuel 16:7).

## BRIAN STERNBERG

What shakes us into seeing God's way? Often it is an event.

Brian Sternberg was good-looking, athletic, and intelligent. He was the most popular man on the campus of the University of Washington. The college guys wanted to be his friend. College girls wanted to date him. Everyone wanted his autograph.

Brian's greatest joy was falling upside down 17 feet above the ground. He was the world champion pole vaulter. In 1963, the Tokyo Olympics were a year away and Brian dreamed of gold.

The expression "His world came crashing down" was literal in Brian's case. Brian's workout routine included using a trampoline to strengthen his legs. He was an expert, confident he needed no spotter to protect him in case of a fall. He lived to regret it. Attempting a double-back somersault with a twist, a move he performed hundreds of times before, he missed. His next conscious moment was on an empty gymnasium floor. At first he thought he was unhurt. He tried to get to his feet. Nothing moved. His body lay still. He cried out for help. No one came.

Hours later, he was discovered and transported to a local hospital. Soon, a surgeon entered his room with the news. Brian was paralyzed. He would never walk again. To Brian, the thought of becoming a quadriplegic was unbearable. But it was easier to contemplate than to face the feelings of what he felt he had lost; Everything.

As he hung suspended and rotated slowly to aid blood flow, his thoughts were all he had left. They were not kind. The injustice of it all shaped him to bitterness. Even in his immovable state he was aware of his depreciating state. Suicide was attractive. But he could not move to do the job.

Soon after the accident, a girl he knew in high school visited his room holding a Bible. She greeted Brian in his hovering state and began to read out loud. Brian gathering barely enough air into his lungs shouted "GET OUT! She did.

The next day she returned to read again. Brian repeated to shoo her from the room. Yet she returned daily to endure his anger and insults. Finally, through his weakened voice, he garnered enough energy to confront: "There is no God! If your God were real, He wouldn't punish me like this! I don't want anything to do with this God of yours…and nothing to do with you!!"

Brian was shocked when she showed up the next day, and every day after. He had met furious competitors before, but nothing like this little woman! Every good athlete knows when it is time to change tactics. "She won't leave," he thought to himself. "Fine. I'll let her blab about Jesus until she finally exhausts herself." It didn't work.

It might have been weeks, perhaps months. One day she entered his room and saw something new in Brian, a calmness. He smiled at her. He explained that a miracle had happened during his evening. Brian had given himself to Christ. Brian, out of options and almost out of hope, surrendered to the only One who could provide any.

Over the next few years, Brian lost his muscular form. He never regained movement. Speaking became possible only with the assistance of a breathing tube. Yet, eventually he became one of the most popular speakers on the Christian circuit. In Baylor University's renowned football coach Grant Taeff's book *I Believe*, he writes;

"The auditorium was totally dark. Suddenly a movie projector lit up and on the screen appeared Brian Sternberg racing down the runway and executing that record-breaking pole vault. Everyone in the audience oohed and aahed.

"Then the auditorium went dark again, except for a single spotlight falling on a single chair on the empty stage. Suddenly out of the shadow on the stage came a huge football player, Wes Wilmer. In his arms he carried Brian Sternberg, crippled. Wilmer placed him on the chair and propped him with pillows to keep him from falling over. Then the raspy voice of Brian Sternberg began to talk: 'My friends, I pray to God that what has happened to me will never happen to any of you. I pray that you will never know the humiliation, the shame of not being able to perform even one human act. It is my hope and my prayer that what has happened to me would never happen to any one of you, UNLESS, my friends, that's what it takes for you to put God in the very center of your life!'"

Through the gritty persistence of a young woman, while rotating within the grasp of cushioned straps, he had time to consider life's eternal questions. God leveraged his brokenness to show him that his purpose was far greater than that of a world-class athlete; to bring God's light into a darkened world.

*Paradigm Shift: "an important change that happens when the usual way of thinking about or doing something is replaced by a new and different way"* [25]

## ROGER BANNISTER

Since 1886, Olympic runners have fantasized about the impossible: running a mile in less than 4 minutes. Like most fantasies, few believed it was possible. Some medical experts felt the human body was not capable. Some claimed that achieving the feat would cause one's internal organs to explode!

But to Roger Bannister, the Four-Minute Mile was a quest he would not deny. For years, he and others consistently failed to reach the mark. In the 1952 Olympics, he attempted a shorter race, finishing in fourth place. Most believed his chances at a four-minute mile were over.

It was time to change his strategy..

---

[25] Merriam-Webster, s.v.: "paradigm shift," accessed November 10, 2024, https://www.meriam-webster.com/dictionary/paradigm-shift

For two months he debated giving up racing. But he could not let go of his vision: To run a sub-four-minute mile.

He changed his workout routine to include brutal interval training. Nearly one year after his Olympic failure, he ran the mile in four minutes, three seconds. "This race made me realize that the four-minute mile was not out of reach," said Bannister.

The following month, he ran the race in 4 minutes and 2 seconds. The following year (1954) in Oxford, England, the impossible materialized. Roger's time was three minutes, fifty-nine and four-tenths of a second.

Roger Bannister's goal of a sub-four-minute mile was not the problem. He needed to change his strategy. He accomplished what others could only dream of by adopting an unconventional training regimen.

Perhaps his greatest achievement was what he did for others. Before Roger Bannister's achievement, Olympic-caliber runners never imagined running a mile in under four minutes. As Bannister crossed the finish line that day in 1954, their paradigm immediately changed. Roger proved it could be done. Over 1,800 runners have now broken the four minute mile barrier.

## GERTRUDE 'TRUDY' EDERLE

Women are weak, incapable of extraordinary athletic achievements. At least, that was the prevailing thought in the 1920s. Thanks to Gertrude 'Trudy' Ederle, that paradigm was about to crumble!

In 1926, Trudy Ederle, a young woman and ex-Olympic swimmer from New Jersey, set out to prove people wrong. The daughter of German immigrants stepped into the chilly waters of Cape Gris-Nez, France to begin her swim to Dover, England.

History was not on her side. Six people had successfully swum the English Channel, all of them men. Almost no one believed a woman could pull it off. It would require a man's muscles and determination to fight the 6-foot waves, and push through schools of stinging jellyfish. The narrowest point between the two nations was 21 miles. A successful swimmer would zig zag across the channel to negotiate the powerful currents, leading to a final swim of about 35 miles.

She was not alone. Boats flanked her while she pushed forward. On her right was her training team, encouraging her and providing nutrition. On her left were boats with reporters sending wireless messages to the shore where radio broadcasters updated listeners.

Although no one knows how many swimmers died attempting to cross the Channel before 1926, one thing is clear: Trudy did not. She found the current in the darkness that would direct her on her final mile to the English shore. Local residents lit fires while tug boats sounded sirens to guide her home. She arrived, her face swollen and bruised by the pounding waves. Salt water had swollen her tongue so much she could barely speak, her body scarred from jellyfish venom. She planted her feet on the wet sand, stood up in waist-deep water, and, guided by the sound of hundreds cheering, walked into her father's waiting arms.

Trudy had swum the English Channel more than 2 hours faster than anyone (men) in history. Two million people lined the streets of New York to celebrate her victory in her ticker-tape parade. A new paradigm was born; Women could accomplish sports greatness!

Soon other women swam the Channel. Women became golf and tennis champions, mountain climbers, race car drivers. Women's sports and businesses today owe much to female champions like Trudy Ederle for shifting the biases that once held them back.

## PIVOT POWER

"Whenever entrepreneurs see a new way to achieve their vision—a way to be more successful —they have to remain nimble enough to take it." Eric Ries, *The Lean Startup*

## THE "GREEN" AISLE.

The world continues to speed up. And it is changing faster every year. The business community knows this.

In the 1980s, the 'low fat' craze hit the grocery stores. Food manufacturers began creating products that promised better health, and the chance to lower people's weight and the risk of heart disease. After focus groups told them that 'green' seemed more organic and healthier, they packed their products in green boxes and containers. Soon, entire grocery store aisles became a long sea of green!

As food science evolved, new data proved that lowering fat was not the answer to weight loss. I realized this after devouring entire boxes of nonfat cookies, each containing over 6 billion calories. Fatter than ever, I moved on. So did many people.

What used to take up an entire store aisle is now a small three-foot section, likely to disappear entirely. (Some customers never learn).

Food companies 'pivoted' to sell their green boxed items to a community hungry for 'low fat.' They pivoted again to serve the same community with 'low carb' foods. I'm waiting for someone to produce the only item I consume that is truly weight-loss friendly; air.

## JOHN WESLEY

John Wesley was trained as an Anglican theologian by the Church of England.

In 1735, he and his brother Charles boarded a ship to America on behest of the governor of Georgia. He hoped to become a minister and evangelist to Native Americans.

While on the ship, there was an enormous storm. It blew off the mast and threatened everyone's life. A group of Moravian missionaries responded to the scene by singing hymns and immersing themselves in prayer. The storm calmed. Wesley recognized it as a work of God.

Wesley stayed in America for two years, yet felt his mission to the natives failed. Depressed, he returned home to England. But he never forgot the inspiration of the Moravians.

While in England, he attended a Moravian service at Aldersgate Street, London. Wesley discovered what he had been seeking, a peace and assurance of his salvation through Christ.

Weeks later he 'pivoted' from his previous messages to a series of sermons on personal salvation by faith. The Methodist movement began.

According to the author Daniel L Burnett, "The significance of Wesley's Aldersgate Experience is monumental. Without it the names of Wesley and Methodism would likely be nothing more than obscure footnotes in the pages of church history."

Not surprisingly, Wesley's new ministry approach was NOT received well by the 'traditionalist' leaders of the Church of England. But with the encouragement of his ole' Oxford friend and evangelist George Whitefield, he found himself 'pivoting' again—preaching NOT in a Church of England but outside in a 'field!'

This was a big deal for Wesley and it conflicted with his Anglican training! Although he was sure his new approach was the best choice, it took him a long while to shake loose the guilt of disregarding what he had been taught. Wesley still harbored feelings that "the saving of souls almost a sin if it had not been done in a church."

After a while, Wesley was pivoting more than a weather vane in a hurricane.

He got even more creative, occasionally using his father's tombstone as his pulpit. I suggest you not try this.

His career spanned 50 years, during which he gave over 40,000 sermons to audiences as large as 20,000. Inside, outside—It didn't matter anymore to good ole' John. He was having the time of his life.

Today, over 75 million people in more than 130 countries identify as Methodists.

John Wesley's teachings spurred the holiness movement leading to the establishment of the Church of the Nazarene, Salvation Army, and several offshoots of Pentecostalism and the Charismatic Movement.

"Men's courses will foreshadow certain ends, to which, if persevered in, they must lead. But if the courses are departed from, the ends must change." —Charles Dickens, *A Christmas Carol*

## COME TO THE TABLE

"When you come to a fork in the road, take it."
—Yogi Berra.

Pastor Mel leads a church in Southeast Washington State. He became concerned when his church began to stagnate. Sundays became predictable: The same people would show up, grab coffee, sing, sit, listen, and leave. He compared the situation to his vision of a thriving church.

A change was needed.

He studied what other churches had done in similar situations. Adding a climbing wall was not an option. Despite being too expensive, the over-60 crowd might fall off. He, of course, could have hired a new worship leader, painted the walls to match the colors of the local college team, shortened his sermons to 12 minutes, or offered the congregation free lottery tickets.

Desperation can work for you or against you. On the negative plane, it can trigger horrible decisions. But it almost always leads us to prayer. Desperate prayer opens our spirit, enabling us to move beyond the fears that hinder innovative ideas.

Mel's prayers were answered with a radical new plan. Mel and his leaders were unsure how the congregation would respond. But the upside was worth the risk.

With the slogan "Come to the Table," the church replaced the linear pews with round tables. The church positioned a staff person at every table. Surprised congregants entered the sanctuary and sat 'in the round.' Mid-way through Mel's sermon, he paused.

Staff members at each table read a short list of discussion questions regarding the sermon such as: "Have you ever had this experience before? What is the most important thing you have learned so far? How can we pray for you?"

After the discussions, Mel would finish the second half of his sermon.

In the conservative town of Kennewick, Washington, this approach was radical. No one was sure it would work, including Mel. Leaders wondered if the congregation would respond positively to it.

Not everyone did. Some left and never returned. But many stayed and celebrated this new approach! Congregants took an active part in discussing the Sunday message. People at the tables began to participate more in mutual prayer. Some who had come to church for years without making connections now had new intimate friends.

You may not have an option to replace your pews with tables. That is not the point. What barriers stand in your way to considering new strategies?

Don't stand in wet cement.

## WHERE'S THE BAR?

I sometimes visit new churches. I always seem to have the same experience. I shake the hand of the greeter and immediately try to find the coffee bar. In many churches, locating the coffee is like searching for the Lost Ark. Tucked into a nondescript area of the lobby in a place where human feet rarely stroll, there is a sweet little lady with a smile. If I'm running late I grab the large silver dispenser to get the last few drops, grab a semi-stale bagel or donut and hustle into the darkened sanctuary just in time for worship.

A church in Idaho was aware of people like me. In addition to their usual coffee counter, they positioned a small five-by-seven-foot coffee bar directly in front of the entrance door. Two smiling people behind the bar welcome you with a free coffee, tea, or a donut. They even pour cream or sweetener into your drink.

What does it cost to do this? A table, two helpful volunteers, and the price of coffee. What is the effect? Church attenders feel cared for. They feel served. Even the nondrinkers appreciate the coffee service, viewing the church as more caring and relational than others. Your small gestures toward your congregation may carry more weight than the educational impact of some of your sermons. (I know. Ouch).

## OUT OF THE LOBBY AND INTO THE SPIRIT

Do you struggle getting everyone to attend the pre-sermon worship in your church? An American church overcame this with a simple solution. They split their worship time in half, with the first half before the sermon and the second half right after.

Immediately following the pastor's final word, the music begins. The room lights remain dim. The congregation gets the message: It is time to worship. The service is not extended, just reformatted to ensure people have a more inspired Sunday experience.

Pivoting is fundamental to our identity as Christians. Jesus calls us to change our ways and alter our course. He challenges us to shift direction, change gears, and turn our lives onto a new path.

Your ability to thrive may depend on your willingness to overcome outdated practices, restrictive paradigms, and success-stifling biases. Perhaps it's time to pivot.

"The pessimist complains about the wind; the optimist expects it to change; the realist adjusts the sails"
—William Arthur Ward

**KEEP IN MIND:**

1. Break Free From Tradition: Move past traditional approaches that keep you anchored in the past.

2. Change Your Paradigm: The willingness to change old paradigms unlocks new ideas.

3. Pivot: Changing your approach is vital to staying relevant in an ever-changing world

Are you prepared to sail past the barriers of old traditions, outdated maps, and the resistance to change? Catching the wind of the two youngest generations is your church's best chance for long-term, sustainable growth. Let's get started!

# PART 3

# REELING IN TOMORROW: HOW TO GET YOUNGER, GROW BIGGER, AND SECURE YOUR FUTURE

One of many things I love about Jesus is His willingness to simplify even the most complex subjects. I especially liked His idea to reduce the 613 Mosaic law commandments to 2.

*"Love the Lord your God with all your heart and with all your soul and with all your mind....Love your neighbor as yourself..."* (Matthew 22:37-40).

Like the Old Testament followers in Jesus' day, modern Christian leaders sometimes act like the hard route is the best one. Maybe we believe that no victory is valid unless we suffer for it. Attempting to grow your church exclusively through adults is not only hard, it is illogical. Grown-ups are not only the most resistant generation, they are the ones with the least number of years left over! The easiest way to achieve long-lasting growth is to flip our evangelistic strategy toward the youngest generation: children.

The next three chapters will not only convince you that children are the 'missing piece' to church growth, they are the most spiritually open and undervalued element of the church.

Chapter 7 will teach you why children are the world's largest under-reached people group, deserving a strategy unique from youth. It will demonstrate that nearly every transformed nation in modern history originated by targeting children.

Chapter 8 will illustrate why children are your greatest evangelism opportunity.

Chapter 9 will explain why children are the most spiritually and mentally prepared to follow Jesus—and the most in need.

## CHAPTER 7

# CASTING YOUR NET IN A WHOLE NEW POND: HOW CHILDREN CAN TRANSFORM YOUR CHURCH

*"If I counted them, they would outnumber the grains of sand... "*
—Psalm 139:18

"We cannot always build the future for our youth, but we can build our youth for the future." —Franklin D. Roosevelt

"*That's when my nightmare began."*

Rwandans, on the morning of April 7, 1994, were jolted awake by terror-induced screams. The horror had begun. And a young girl's life was forever changed.

"My name is Gift. I remember the day when my life turned upside down.

I woke up to the news that somebody had assassinated our president. He belonged to the Hutu tribe. Some Hutus blamed the Tutsi tribe for the murder. It was a devastating time, with men mercilessly targeting anyone who might be Tutsi, including me and my family.

*That's when my nightmare began. My family and I were targeted to be killed. Men, women, and children were hunted down, brutally attacked with machetes, and systematically shot. It was so violent and brutal. My family and I knew our only escape was to walk 60 miles to the Democratic Republic of Congo with other Tutsis.*

*We walked very far through dangerous jungles. We had nothing to eat and no sense of direction. There were constant storms. There was no hiding from the relentless downpour, no shield from the horrible heat. We were constantly exhausted and became very weak. I remember my legs swelling. We were quickly running out of water and food.*

*As we pushed through the dense jungles, I watched many of my friends and neighbors die including my brother and my cousin.*

*We finally arrived at a Congolese refugee camp. But we only stayed for a short while. We needed to leave because people were dying from dysentery. We decided to walk through a Congolese jungle and try to make it to Kenya.*

*We survived on leaves and water, but due to the grace of God, we arrived in Kenya. Everyone in my family was traumatized. I was so sad and heartbroken, driven into depression from the misery in my life. Each night I was tormented by nightmares. I would dream about my friends and relatives who died during the war. Their voices reached out to me, pleading for help. But I couldn't help. Sometimes they shouted for me to escape from the violent attackers armed with machetes and guns.*

*I had nowhere to turn. So, amid this sadness, I surrendered my life to Jesus. Soon He replaced my trauma with His overwhelming peace. My parents were opposed to my being a born-again Christian, but I knew it was the right thing for me.*

*You see, I couldn't escape Jesus's love. Experiencing the Word of God, connecting with Him in prayer, and worshiping with fellow believ-*

ers brought me the peace I craved in my spirit. Finally, I was able to sleep through the night.

God eventually blessed me with marriage. My husband and I moved to Burundi. I began to pray daily that God would empower me and show me how to assist others who are suffering through similar traumatic experiences. Soon, a pastor introduced me to the thinkSMALL Burundi team. I began helping them to train children how to protect themselves from traffickers and abusers. I learned how to share the Gospel and disciple them for Jesus.

Serving in thinkSMALL revitalized my spirit and helped me recognize my life's purpose. When I share my story, I see its effect on people who are struggling. When they hear me talk about how God saved me, they also want to receive Jesus.

Violence, abuse, and exploitation break a child's spirit. But Jesus can heal them with His overwhelming love. No one can take away the hope He gives to them.

I believe that there was a higher power guiding me during the intense trials of war and the unimaginable atrocities of genocide. Jesus is the One who shaped me into the leader I am today."

Gift's story is shared worldwide as a testimony of God's strength and willingness to use even the most horrific experiences to inspire hope in others. Through her leadership, thousands of young Burundians are now following the Lord.

In this chapter, we will discuss why children are the strategic answer to growing your church and ensuring its long-term sustainability. We will explore why using standard generational labels, like Gen Z, are insufficient for your church. We'll dive into why children under 15 should be considered an under-reached people group. Finally, we will look at a less-known scripture that answers the question: What steps are needed to achieve a transformed church and nation? Are they still relevant for today?

## GENERATION AGITATION

When will it all end? Gen Z, Gen Y, Gen X, Baby Boomers, The 'Silent' Generation, The G.I. Generation (no these are not military veterans). It's enough to make your head spin.

This whole 'Gen craze' began in the late 1900s. Academics, marketing execs, and national governments decided to label groups of people based on birth years. The assumption is that people born between a specific range of years have a similar worldview, interests, and perhaps favorite desserts. Marketers tailor products, music, entertainment, education, politics, and religion to fit the designated generation.

You have heard a lot about Gen Z. Who are they? Dictionaries cannot even agree! The Merriam-Webster Online Dictionary describes Generation Z as "the generation of people born in the late 1990s and early 2000s." The Collins Dictionary defines them as "born between the mid-1990s and mid-2010s who are seen as confident users of new technology". What about the unconfident? Or the users of old technology? Should we create a new generation just for them?

Are Gen Z'ers living in a poor area of Ethiopia or a mountain tribe in Thailand the same as those in America? It's easy to overthink this, isn't it?

Whoever they are, they must be important. We hold conferences for them, camps for them, mission trips for them, worship services for them.

If Generation Z refers to those born before about 2010, who are those born afterward?

## WELCOME GENERATION A!

Mark McCrindle, a generational researcher and consultant in Australia, invented the term Generation A in 2005. Generation A refers to the kids born between 2010 and 2025. Labeled "screenagers," they were born during the introductions of the iPad and Instagram, with their minds and worldview greatly influenced by the screen.

There is something all Gen Z and Gen A people have in common; They get older. Once that happens we must invent a whole new label. I can't wait, can you?

## CHILDREN: THE WORLD'S LARGEST UNDER-REACHED PEOPLE GROUP

Jesus authorized His disciples to 'go and disciple the nations' (Matthew 28:19). The nations Jesus referred to were ethnic groups. Today's most common term for them is people groups. There are between 17,000 to 24,000 people groups around the world.

The Joshua Project and Global Frontier track people groups worldwide. Frontier defines people groups this way: "…the largest group through which the Gospel can flow without encountering significant barriers of understanding and acceptance. In other words, *a people group calls "us, us" and "them, them"* by distinguishing insiders and outsiders." Most people groups share a familiar location, language, religion, ethnicity, culture, or some other vital features. According to the Joshua Project, 42 percent of the groups are unreached, with less than 3 percent of the population as Jesus followers.

If you ever want to stump people in a trivia contest, ask them what nation reaches the most people groups. It is not the United States, nor South Korea. India leads the world by sending missionaries to 2,279 people groups within its own nation!

There are roughly 370,000 children born in the world each day. Every year that number increases. What we do to reach and influence this generation will determine our nations, communities and churches.

Children under age 15 make up 25 percent of the global population. They speak different languages, come from other cultures, and share different religions. And because of their cognitive and psychological similarities I have chosen to add them to the list of 'people groups.'

Despite the great work of the Joshua Project, no group has tracked the global percentage of children following Christ. Based on our experience with over 3,000 churches in Asia, Africa, and the Americas, I estimate it's under 5 percent.

Compassion International estimates that only 3 percent of the average church budget goes toward children. This underreached people group is the most vulnerable, unprotected, and moldable group in your community. Catch this group for Christ and the future of your church will change.

## THE OVERLOOKED SCRIPTURE THAT CAN SAVE YOUR CHURCH

In 2006, I was a missionary in Thailand. I started a ministry called ETCB (Evangelism Through Church Business) to help churches create businesses like coffee shops and beauty parlors, supporting the church and building relationships with unbelievers. ETCB aimed to reach adults for Christ and disciple them in church. The businesses were more successful than the evangelism. Business as a Mission is a great ministry, but I was looking for a faster way to grow the Kingdom of God.

I needed a Biblical strategy to quickly grow churches, expand God's Kingdom and work effectively in today's modern world. It needed to be simple, teachable, and multipliable. After months of prayer and frustration I found it.

At first, I hesitated. It seemed too simple. (Perhaps that is why I missed it so many times before). I assumed that if something was going to be impactful, it had also to be complex. I mean, that is what my college professors seem to say.

Here are the scriptures from Psalms 78:4-8, written by David's worship leader Asaph.

4 *"We will not hide these truths from our children; we will tell the next generation about the glorious deeds of the Lord, about his power and his mighty wonders."*

Interpretation = Child Evangelism. (Asaph understood that reaching children for God was the essential first step in transforming his nation).

5 *"For he issued his laws to Jacob; he gave his instructions to Israel. He commanded our ancestors to teach them to their children, 6 so the next generation might know them—even the children not yet born— and they in turn will teach their own children. 7 So each generation should set its hope anew on God, not forgetting his glorious miracles and obeying his commands."*

Interpretation = Child Discipleship. (Asaph encouraged Israel to disciple two successive generations of children).

8 *"Then they will not be like their ancestors— stubborn, rebellious, and unfaithful, refusing to give their hearts to God."*

Interpretation; National Transformation. (Asaph recognized that transforming Israel would come not come through the 'stubborn, rebellious, and unfaithful' adult generation, but from a generation of God-fearing children).

Jesus had a similar message: *"But Jesus called the children to him and said, "Let the little children come to me, and do not hinder them, for the kingdom of God belongs to such as these."* (Luke 18:16)

There is no indication Asaph was a "children's minister," nor Sunday School teacher. It's hard to know if he even liked kids. It made no difference. He understood what it would take to rebuild his nation.

At first glance, Asaph's strategy seems improbable. My first reaction was to laugh it off as old-fashioned. How could a strategy written 3,000 years ago be relevant for today? I decided to investigate.

## CHINA

Zedong ruled China from 1949 to 1976. He was born on a farm in 1893 in Hunan province, the son of prosperous peasants. While working at Peking University as a librarian he was exposed to Marxist-Leninism. Mao believed it could free Chinese citizens from poverty. But like other atheist doctrines it guarantees a repressive totalitarian state.

In 1919, when Mao Zedong started teaching history at a primary school, he persuaded students to demonstrate against the Hunan provincial governor, who was well-known for his oppressive and brutal treatment of people. Mao's impact on youth expanded quickly. He co-authored a revolutionary monthly journal available to students and less educated people, further spreading his ideas.

In the end, Mao led students in toppling the dictatorial governor, which led to his appointment as the director of the country's most important school—a critical position that played an essential role in sparking the communist revolution.

He eventually published what is famously called his "Little Red Book," simple enough for children to read. Millions did. His popularity with children spread from cities to farmlands. In time, they elevated him to lead the nation.

In 1949, Mao implemented his communist vision by founding the People's Republic of China.

Did Mao teach the children every detail of communism? No. He didn't need to. He inspired them with a vision. He was kind to them. He promised them a new world. They followed him until they discovered his promises were in vain. By that time, it was too late.

The people rose in protest as Mao Zedong's shared economy plans failed time and time again, causing economic catastrophe and widespread starvation. Once again, Mao sought support from the younger generation. He closed schools and organized a paramilitary squad called the Red Guards, consisting of children and youth. The Red Guards' mission was to brutally enforce Mao's commands by abusing or murdering everyone who dared to oppose him. This campaign was part of the Cultural Revolution and its mission to eradicate capitalism and traditional values from Chinese society. Mao's use of young fanatics to stifle opposition strengthened his grip on power. Mao Zedong led the nation for 27 years, dying in 1976.

## VIETNAM

Ho Chi Mihn was a children's teacher and a disciple of Mao Zedong. Vietnamese children affectionately referred to him as "Uncle Ho." He was kind. Children loved him. Eventually he raised an army, many of whom were children. They were willing to fight to the death for Uncle Ho. Many did.

In April, 1975, the final battle in Saigon chased nearly 150,000 terrified people from the nation before, many being flown from the rooftop of the Saigon Hotel.

## SOVIET UNION

Vladimir Lenin, the founder of the Soviet Union (1917-1924) understood the importance of influencing children. He proudly proclaimed "Give me a child for the first 5 years of his life and he will be mine forever."

## IRAN

Iran has a long history of indoctrination in primary schools.

Brigade General Mohammad-Saleh Jokar of Iran oversees the Basij student militia. There are 6,000 "resistance centers" in elementary schools, preparing students to join military units when they transfer to middle schools at age 12.

According to Jokar, "schoolchildren are more susceptible at a young age than at any other time in their lives...and we want to promote and instill into elementary schoolchildren the ideas of the revolution..."

Iranian children who resist are sent to "psychology centers" for reform and re-education. Many are beaten and subject to psychological torture.

Iran's authorities are fervently committed to indoctrinating children, believing it as critical to retaining power. They aim to mold the younger generation›s views and devotion through implementing their ideology into the school system and youth programs early on, ensuring ongoing support for those in power.

Religious education is a crucial component emphasizing Shiite Islamic tenets. This religious framework supports the political system by combining religion and devotion to the state.

By focusing on the children, Iranian officials aim to ensure an ideologically committed population, guaranteeing their dominance in the future. The strategy of early indoctrination plays a vital role in sustaining the regime's stability and authority.

## NORTH KOREA

North Korea indoctrinates children at an early age. The government regularly removes youngsters as young as three, four, or five years old and subjects them to severe indoctrination for up to one year. Children learn to revere the government, especially the "Great Leader," through strict education, games, and music.

Children are eventually returned to their families as "converted," listed as unofficial estate agents, reporting any opposition within their families or communities.

## NAZI GERMANY

The Hitler Youth (Hitlerjugend) was launched in 1926, 7 years before Adolf Hitler took control of the government. Once in power, he banned the Boy Scouts. The Hitlerjugend became mandatory in 1939 for boys between 14 to 18. Millions of boys were indoctrinated with Nazi ideology and trained for future military duty.

Parallel to the Hitlerjugend was the League of German Girls (Bund Deutscher Mädel). Girls were indoctrinated with Nazi ideology and trained in physical fitness and obedience to prepare them for roles in the regime and as future mothers.

Hitler understood that mobilizing the younger generations was essential to his movement's future, stating in his book *Mein Kampf,*" Whoever has the youth has the future."

The Hitler Youth and his League of German Girls received extensive international publicity. What was less known is Hitler's dedication to recruit and indoctrinate young children.

In 1936, the German Reich Youth Office required German boys aged 10 to register. Those identified as racially acceptable (Aryan) were expected to join the Jungvolk (The Young People). This organization prepared children for entry into the Hitler Youth by age fourteen.

The Jungvolk taught boys the principles of Naziism, including racial purity and obedience to Hitler. Educational materials and activities stressed discipline, bravery, and solidarity. Children participated in rallies, marches, and ceremonies honoring key Nazi leaders.

In his book *Life and Death in the Third Reich*, Peter Fritzsche wrote that Hitler viewed the Jungvolk as an important element of raising a national army.

"...after four years of the Young Folk (Jungvolk), they go on to the Hitler Youth, where we have them for another four years ... And even if they are still not complete National Socialists, they go to the Labor Service and are smoothed out there for another six, seven months ... And whatever class consciousness or social status might still be left ... the Wehrmacht *(armed forces)* will take care of that."

Children are a key in creating and strengthening power for oppressors like Mao Zedong, Ho Chi Mihn, Kim Jong Un, Adolf Hitler, Iran, and other Islamic nations. Revolutions may topple governments but are rarely long-lasting. A nation's transformation depends on raising a young generation to carry shared values into adulthood and eventually become the country's influencers.

Asaph was right. Discipling and mobilizing a population of children is the key to transforming nations, but what about a more positive story?

Most people identify South Korea as a Christian nation. But few are aware of children's crucial role in making this happen.

## SOUTH KOREA

In 1945 only 2 percent of South Koreans were Christian.[26] After the Korean War, South Korea was one of the poorest countries in Asia, agricultural and predominantly Buddhist. Christian leaders, struggling to bring the hope of Christ to the country, united across denominations and decided to target their efforts on children. Gin building schools, offering religious education, and freely sharing the Gospel. The nation's Christian population surged from 2 percent to over 35 percent within one generation.

Christianity breeds leadership. In time, more than 60 percent of South Korean government leaders proclaimed Jesus as Lord, enacting fair and compassionate laws.

Churches continued to grow. Christian business leaders invested time and resources toward community needs of education, and social problems. Their contributions dramatically influenced the nation's growth. Christians and non-Christians reaped the benefits. Today (2024), despite its small size, South Korea has the fourth-largest economy in Asia, trailing only China, Japan, and India.

*"Blessed is the nation whose God is the LORD, the people he chose for his inheritance"* (Psalm 33:12).

Will it last? Sadly, as in the West, there has been an increasing attraction to secularism in the country. "The younger generation is leaving the church in startling fashion," said Steven Chang, a New Testament professor in Seoul. The reasons are complex, ranging from

---

[26] The Economist; "Why South Korea is so distinctively Christian"; https://www.economist.com/the-economist-explains/2014/08/12/why-south-korea-is-so-distinctively-christian

Western secularization, to materialism, to high-profile corruption in the church.

But those young people are also a source of hope. "There are signs of younger churches and church leaders who are leaving the mega-church, prosperity-Gospel, gift-oriented ministry models and going back to the simple Gospel message," Chang said.

One thing is clear. What will drive the global church forward (or in reverse) is influenced by the youngest generations. Don't overlook them. Empower them!

*[27] Instead, God chose things the world considers foolish in order to shame those who think they are wise. And he chose things that are powerless to shame those who are powerful.* 1 Cor 1:27

To spiritually renew our nation, we must inspire enough new young Jesus-followers to create a movement. History, and God's Word, proves it.

### KEEP IN MIND:

1. Children have always been the key to transforming nations around the world.

2. Children represent the world's largest untapped mission field.

3. The future of the church depends on reaching and empowering the two youngest generations (Psalms 78:4-8).

*"Come, follow me, ...and I will send you out to fish for people."* Matthew 4:19

Are you missing out on hundreds of smaller fish while patiently waiting for the big one? Look down. They are swimming next to your boat. In the upcoming chapter, we'll fish out the reasons why hauling in minnows (children) will have more impact on your church than reeling in the occasional marlin!

## CHAPTER 8

# FISHING ON THE RIGHT SIDE OF YOUR BOAT: NETTING CHILDREN, SECURING YOUR FUTURE

6 *"He said, 'Throw your net on the right side of the boat and you will find some.' When they did, they were unable to haul the net in because of the large number of fish."*
—John 21:6

"If I could relive my life, I would devote my entire ministry to reaching children for God."
—D.L. Moody

## FISHING LESSONS (PART 1)

Nothing is more frustrating than being the hardest-working unproductive member of the team.

Peter may have felt that way; fishing all night without a bite! Exhausted. Discouraged. A bit irritated. Knowing Peter's personality, I can only imagine his initial reaction when a stranger on the shore shouted unsolicited advice.

Jesus was enjoying His morning walk on the beach when a thought crossed his mind: "Breakfast!" Grilled fish sounded good. I can imagine Him smiling, shaking His head as He looked out toward the boat. Fishermen packed the vessel, exhausted and burning from the morning sun. Despite the blinding glare reflecting off the water, Jesus could easily see the disappointment in their tired faces. They, on the other hand, could not recognize Him. When He yelled out "How's the fishing?" He already knew the answer.

The men had been up all night. It's a mystery why they responded to His question. After all, what did He know about fishing? Besides, it was a dumb question. Every fisherman knew that the best fishing was in the evening. But there was something unique about this stranger on the shore. He spoke with authority. Instructing them to "Throw the net on the right side of the boat" They felt an irresistible urge to obey. After all, what did they have to lose?

The rest is history. Lots of fish. Lots of breakfast. Lots of Jesus. But a significant lesson as well. Perhaps our traditional way of fishing (for people) needs to be reexamined. Is it time to throw your nets on the other side of the boat?

This chapter will examine how and why we often miss the ultimate catch for the Kingdom, the children.

## MARLIN OR MINNOWS

Flathead minnows are freshwater fish about 2" in length. They swim in lakes, ponds, and rivers throughout North America. If you are hungry, you could eat a pound of them, about 220 fish! In contrast, an average adult blue marlin typically reaches about 11 feet long and weighs between 200 and 400 pounds.

You must travel to catch a marlin, unless you live near the warm tropical waters of the Indian, Pacific, or Atlantic oceans. You probably need to hire a boat and a guide. Despite all this, you have only a

9 percent chance of catching one (and if you do, good luck getting it home in your car).

If you are lucky enough to hook a blue or white marlin, hauling it into your boat can take 3 or more hours. The good news is that you will have bragging rights. You will feel proud. You'll show off the photo of you standing proudly by your prize catch. You'll post it online. You may even have the fish stuffed and hung on your living room wall (to your wife's delight).

Catching a flathead minnow? Pretty easy. Launch your boat, drop your net, and haul them in. No big struggle. Less bragging rights. No photo necessary. Hanging your prize minnow on the wall will not impress anyone. Unless they bring their binoculars, they won't even see it!

But what if catching a minnow turned you on as much (or more) as hooking a marlin? What if each small fish caught brought more long-term value to your church than the 'harder to catch' big one? Strategically speaking, which one would you choose? Children, the minnows of the world, are swimming in mass right next to your boat!

While most church leaders are marlin fishing, another boat is fishing in your waters, led by a seasoned fisherman and crew. They have been harvesting God's sea since the dawn of time. While you hold a pole, they throw a net. While you struggle to bring in one marlin, they haul in thousands of minnows.

The devil's goal is to destroy God's church, including yours. Children are his most valued catch. Non-Christian children eventually become parents of non-Christian children who influence their peers, redefine cultural values, reshape communities and jeopardize the future of the church.

Don't give up on adults. But if you want to secure the long-term future, children are your only answer.

There are roughly 8 billion people worldwide. Two billion are children under 15. Over 90 percent (est) of them do not know Christ. Why? Nobody has told them.

"...And how can they believe in him if they have never heard about him? And how can they hear about him unless someone tells them?" (Romans 10:14)

## WHAT HOLDS YOU BACK?

One of the craziest things a leader can say is, "I'm not a children's person." That is a bit like a carpenter saying "I'm not a hammer person." When you need a hole, you suddenly realize you might be.

Before 2007, I also claimed not to be a 'children's person.' Frankly, they rarely crossed my mind. I didn't hate them. I valued kids as general principal, valuable contributors toward growing the human population. I have never been a father. The closest I came to playing with kids was wrestling with my nephew on the floor. But he was 20 at the time.

Despite my preference for adults, I made the difficult decision to step out of my comfort zone. My wife and I launched thinkSMALL Global Ministries in 2007. Our indigenous teams lead church youth teams into communities to train children how to resist trafficking, abuse, internet exploitation, and drug use. The ministry now serves 20 nations including the United States. Over 1.3 million non-believers have come to Christ with more than 71 percent entering church discipleship. Not because of me, but because of our implementing and customizing Jesus' Kingdom growth strategies.

Churches have grown. And, surprisingly, I've grown to love children...which is a great shock to me and an even bigger one to my wife, Paula.

Your comfort zone is irrelevant if you are serious about achieving the best results. When all is said and done you have two choices; You can do what's uncomfortable until it becomes comfortable, or you can delegate it to others. Either is fine. But you should never choose the easier, less effective solution!

## CONFIRMATION BIAS

In Chapter 6, I wrote about the barriers that hinder you from choosing the most effective strategies. Concerning children, confirmation bias becomes one of those barriers.

Confirmation bias is choosing information that aligns with our beliefs yet ignoring information that does not. Below are five common beliefs that leaders often hold, despite contrary evidence. These wrong beliefs become a magnetic force pulling you away from the steps needed to reach and nurture your youngest generation for Christ. They can also prevent you from doing what is necessary to build the long-term future of your church.

## CONFIRMATION BIAS #1: IN THE EYES OF GOD, AN ADULT SAVED IS MORE VALUABLE THAN A CHILD.

The disciples thought so.

Now and then, we say the right thing at the right time. For Jesus, it was always the right thing. He was just about to arrive in Jerusalem. The crowd was waiting, excited to hear what He had to say. He pushed through the crowd to the front. The crush of people pressed against each other to get a better view of this great Healer, Teacher, and self-proclaimed Messiah. Everyone was jostling for position to catch a glimpse of and possibly touch the skin of this 'rock star' of religion.

Parents tried to approach Jesus with their children, hoping for a blessing from the touch of His hand. The disciples jumped in. "Hey, get those kids out of here! He's got no time for that!" they might have shouted (Luke 18:15). Jesus ended the chaos immediately. He blessed the children and gave them a free ticket to the front row! Then, He delivered one of His most essential teachings to the amazed crowd;

*"Let the little children come to me, and do not hinder them, for the kingdom of God belongs to such as these"* (Luke 18:16).

Keeping children from Jesus is offensive to the Father. Delaying the opportunity to know Christ denies them access to the One who can meet their deepest spiritual needs.

Jesus highlights the importance of children and uses them as an example to show what is required to enter His Kingdom.

*17 "I tell you the truth, anyone who doesn't receive the Kingdom of God like a child will never enter it"* (Luke 18:17).

To drive the point home to His disciples, He implied that neglecting to serve children could result in missing out on God's blessings.

*42 "And if anyone gives even a cup of cold water to one of these little ones who is my disciple, truly I tell you, <u>that person will certainly not lose their reward</u>"* (Matthew 10:42).

## CONFIRMATION BIAS #2: IT IS WRONG TO EVANGELIZE CHILDREN. IT IS MANIPULATIVE AND DOES NOT RESPECT THEIR RIGHTS TO CHOOSE THEIR PATH.

The enemy loves this one. God sees it differently.

*4"We will not hide these truths from our children; we will tell the next generation about the glorious deeds of the Lord, about his power and his mighty wonders."* (Psalm 78:4)

Satan is an evangelist, heavily focused on children. He is clothed in lies. His plan is to influence local culture, and change the course of history by winning over the hearts and minds of the youngest generation.

## CONFIRMATION BIAS #3: CHILDREN ARE UNABLE TO UNDERSTAND THE GOSPEL.

Children can understand the Gospel by age 4. Jesus made the Gospel simple so that anyone could grasp it. Adults, on the other hand, complicate it. Children are spiritually equipped to connect with God in ways that adults often struggle.

[25] *"At that time Jesus said, 'I praise you, Father, Lord of heaven and earth, because you have hidden these things from the wise and learned, and revealed them to little children'"* (Matthew 11:25).

## CONFIRMATION BIAS #4: CHILDREN'S BRAINS ARE UNDEVELOPED AND ILL-EQUIPPED TO UNDERSTAND THEOLOGY.

I could say the same for many adults.

Children may not fully grasp some of the deeper theological elements of the Bible. They may struggle to accurately recite the original 613 Mosaic commandments (who can?).

But kids are very good at reciting Jesus' biggest hits ('Love the Lord your God with all your heart and with all your soul and with all your mind...and 'Love your neighbor as yourself.')

And they can set the example for adults in this one:

*"A new command I give you: Love one another. As I have loved you, so you must love one another"* (John 13:34).

## CONFIRMATION BIAS #5: AMERICAN (OR WESTERN) CULTURE AND LAWS PROHIBIT CHILD EVANGELISM.

Laws may prohibit religious messages in government-operated locations, such as public schools. But there are many other places where children congregate in your area.

Churches and other Christian-operated organizations are filled with children that have yet to embrace Jesus as Lord. Preschools and elementary schools are 'deep wells' filled with children seeking what

Jesus can offer. These leaders are often willing to allow your church to bring a message of hope and salvation to these children.

Opportunities may exist in privately owned apartment buildings, children's hospitals, section 8 communities, community centers, and public parks. Parking lot events, skits, sports camps, children's hospitals, and other locations are available. Many small towns in the United States are open to child evangelism in public places, sometimes even within public schools.

Shed your restrictive thinking. Pray, brainstorm, and seek out the openings in your community to reach this critical generation. The enemy is fishing in your pond. Beat him at his own game!

Fish with a net. And throw it on the other side of your boat!

## FISHING LESSONS (PART 2)

Despite the global population growth, there is a declining percentage of 'minnows' in the sea.

In 1950, children under the age of 15 comprised 35 percent of the world's population. In 2022, it fell to 25 percent.

Some global influences include the increased availability of birth control and abortions. In the United States, abortions take the lives of about 1 million babies per year. Even in nations where abortions are illegal, there are an increasing number performed. In many countries people are marrying later, shortening the time when women are capable of birth. Economies may make children less affordable and force women in poor communities into the workplace. In the Western World, women may choose careers over large families.

What can we conclude? There may be legitimate reasons for smaller families. But if children are the most spiritually hungry segment of the world's population, the key to our future, yet shrinking in population size, we must reach them now!

Despite the emotional rewards of landing the biggest fish, we have little time to waste. Be a professional fisherman. Use every tool at your disposal. Equip yourself to succeed in as short a time as possible. Get the most fish into your net and haul them aboard your boat now. The future of your church may depend on it.

## TRANSFORMATION OF AN AMERICAN CHURCH (TEXAS)

"Anyone who is not sowing into the next generation is automatically sowing into obsolescence."—Pastor Cere Muscarella, Life Foursquare Church

Pastor Cere Muscarella leads a successful Angleton, Texas church. He built the church using his denomination's traditional methods. Stagnated, he thought the model required 'juice.' He shifted his strategy to a 'two generations down' approach, wanting a church that maximized its impact now and into the future.

"In the beginning our congregation was excited about the new vision. But as soon as we began spending much money on it, some pushed back." Does that sound familiar?

Pastor Cere got bold, telling his congregation, "We adults are saved already! The Kingdom is not about us. It's about finding where the battle is raging and meeting that with all available resources. The Battle is for the lives of our kids!"

Cere continued to share the vision until even the resistors gave up their fight. He said "You can't have a successful children's ministry without changing the minds and hearts of the people who pay the bills. Anyone who is NOT sowing into the next generation is sowing into OBSOLESCENCE. You will not survive what's coming without reaching down RIGHT NOW to the young generations."

The church rebranded itself as youth focused. Over time, the congregation grew both spiritually and financially. His church currently boasts 13 buildings—11 of them for kids!

[21] *"Wherever your treasure is, there the desires of your heart will also be"* (Matthew 6:21).

Pastor Cere concluded, "If Senior Pastors want to get these great results, they must be the first to buy in!"

## TRANSFORMATION OF AN AMERICAN CHURCH (WASHINGTON)

Craig dreamed of becoming a missionary. As a young man, the idea of serving the Lord in foreign nations was so powerful he was certain it came from God. Emotionally, he was ready to pack his bags. One day his plans were interrupted by an invitation to pastor a small church. Little did he know that his 'yes' decision would lead him to a lifetime of church leadership. He recently retired after pastoring a thriving church in Spokane, Washington for 32 years. Sometimes God knows best.

Pastor Craig always had a heart for kids. He challenged his leaders to establish a ministry to feed underprivileged kids in Spokane, and bring them into church. This ministry became key to how he reaches kids and helps them grow as followers and future leaders in his church and community.

As kids began to flow to his church, Craig realized he needed to revamp the children's department. Not satisfied to merely make his church 'kid-friendly,' he determined to make it 'kid-inviting.' He commissioned a team to remodel a large section of the church building to become a destination area...a place where kids would run to, rather than be dragged into, on Sunday mornings. The bold colored hallway to the kids' rooms features cool artwork kids can't resist. The rooms shine with bright, fun colors as if to say "Jesus is here. Jesus is cool. Jesus is FUN!"

Children's teachers educate children with engaging yet spiritually challenging curricula, preparing them as young champions for Christ. Kids develop a submissive and intimate relationship with Christ as they learn to maximize their potential as future influencers.

Craig looked at me recently, and said, "You know, Gary, there is no place in the Bible where God tells children to be more like an adult."

*"Truly I tell you, unless you change and become like little children, you will never enter the kingdom of heaven"* (Matthew 18:3).

## IT'S NOT ALL BAD

There is a positive trend happening. Churches are waking up to the urgent need to invest resources into children. Ministry Architects surveyed over 1,000 American churches reporting churches are beginning to invest more of their budget into their children's ministry.[27]

Budgeting is tough. You are overwhelmed with financial requests. It is easy to invest additional funds into adult or youth programs. Some of these programs are essential. Weigh your opportunities and investments carefully. Consider your long-term vision and ask yourself what is more essential than securing the future of your church? Don't risk the future for today. Many churches fail when they make the mistake of stepping over dollars to pick up pennies.

[21] *"Wherever your treasure is, there the desires of your heart will also be"* (Matthew 6:21).

## IT'S TIME TO LET DOWN YOUR NET

[5] *"Simon answered, 'Master, we've worked hard all night and haven't caught anything. But because you say so, I will let down the nets.'* [6] *When*

---

[27] Ministry Architects Stats Children's Ministry Norms and Statistics; https://ministryarchitects.com/childrens-ministry-norms/

*they had done so, they caught such a large number of fish that their nets began to break.*" (Luke 5:5-6).

Soon Simon remembered what Jesus taught him 3 years earlier. The miracle wasn't about fish after all. "*Follow Me, and I will make you fishers of men*" (Matthew 4:19).

It is time to let down your net to reach the most plentiful fish in the sea. Go after the minnows. They will grow into bigger fish. And your nation, community and, yes, your church, will experience a new spirit of transformation.

### KEEP IN MIND:

1. Children are your biggest opportunity for long-term growth and security.
2. Reaching children may require a shift in evangelistic strategy.
3. Catching minnows (children) is less challenging and often more fruitful than catching marlins (adults).

How do you catch children for Christ? You need to know how they think. Don't skip the next chapter! It's the anchor point for choosing your best path forward.

## CHAPTER 9

# HOOKED ON HOPE: WHY KIDS RUN TO CHRIST AND ADULTS RUN AWAY

[25] *"At that time Jesus said, 'I praise you, Father, Lord of heaven and earth, because you have hidden these things from the wise and learned, and revealed them to little children.'"*
—Matthew 11:25

"It's easier to build strong children than to repair broken men...cheaper too."
—Frederick Douglas

"They're just not biting." Ah, the fisherman's lament. You can use the best equipment and technique and still get nothing. You can change your bait or fish at a different time of day and still get the same results. Not a nibble.

As the comedian Steven Wright once said, "There's a fine line between fishing and just standing on the shore like an idiot!"

## THE AGE OF ACCOUNTABILITY

India's population has more than doubled since 1950. In 2023, it grew by another 11 million. Only 2.5 percent of Indians are Christian. Due to the population growth that percentage continues to fall.

In 2018, I shared the critical mission of reaching children for Christ with 20 pastors in Kolkata, India. In turn I needed to understand their evangelism strategies.

Springtime in Kolkata can be scorching. This day was no different and I was nervous. I had written a presentation to encourage 22 Indian pastors to reach children for Christ. As I stood before these pastors, I could almost read their minds. I was a foreigner who knew little about India and less about their churches. As my talk began, they responded politely. But they were skeptical. They had never considered child evangelism as a strategy before.

These pastors were committed followers of Christ. But they were disheartened by India's widespread opposition to Christianity. Another obstacle was the Indian national government, which safeguarded the Hindu majority by enacting an anti-conversion statute.

Most pastors seemed to doubt India ever becoming a Christian nation.

Five minutes into the meeting I asked them, "At what age do you feel it is appropriate to introduce the Gospel?" Their unanimous response was, "18!" They believed that children ought to mature to an "age of accountability," where they could carefully weigh their religious options and come to a conscious, definitive decision.

I explained that most people (especially children) come to Christ, not through a careful intellectual analysis but through an unmet spiritual need for hope. For several of the pastors, this simple message was a breakthrough.

They began to partner with our two Indian teams reaching out to children in their local communities. Churches grew and became younger. The ministry grew exponentially as pastors shared their newly discovered strategies and successes until 476 congregations joined in. More than 29,000 children became believers over the next six years, with 83 percent of them entering into discipleship.

Many of these children are now youth leaders, guiding their friends to Jesus. They will soon be the next generation of parents, pastors, and community leaders.

The pastors overcame their antiquated church traditions and biases about children. After years of catching only an occasional marlin, they pivoted and threw their nets over the 'right side' of their boat to haul in 29,000 minnows!

This chapter will reveal why focusing solely on adults is an ineffective approach, particularly if your goal is to secure the long-term future of your church.

## EVANGELIZING ADULTS: TIMING IS EVERYTHING

Have you ever wondered why convincing adults to follow Christ is so difficult?

It is usually about timing. Adults are less willing to change their belief system unless experiencing a crisis that forces them to reevaluate their lives. Crisis shakes our confidence, softens our hearts, and causes us to ask life's most important questions. Tragedies such as a broken marriage, the death of a loved one, the loss of a job, the torment of alcoholism, drugs, or marital abuse can pry open resistant minds towards Christ.

In comfortable seasons of life, adults are less willing to change. Many have built close relationships with non-believing friends and family and are unwilling to jeopardize them. Seeds scattered on hardened soil may not grow roots until some rain comes along and softens it up.

## EVANGELIZING YOUTH: FRIENDS ARE KEY

Most evangelism events today are geared toward youth. Church camps, outreaches, and concerts for teenagers are on the rise, drawing thousands to the Lord. But how many take the next step into church? And, of the ones that do, how many remain after one year?

Most teenagers are insecure, leaning on friends to provide that security. In the early stages of their walk with Christ, they are vulnerable to being pulled back into their original friendship groups.

## NO CRAB LEFT BEHIND

In Boston, a man was walking along a fishing dock. He looked down and noticed a bucket of crabs. He wondered why there was no lid to keep them inside. After all, he thought, the crabs will likely escape.

He watched for a while and noticed that a crab would occasionally attempt to climb to the top of the bucket. Each time it approached the edge, another crab would reach up its claws and pull it back down! Soon another crab attempted to escape, but met the same fate. One by one, crabs would work their way toward the top of the bucket and be yanked back down. The crab fisherman needed no lid to keep his crabs from leaving the bucket. The other crabs would take care of that themselves.

Human beings are similar. In behavioral science, this conduct became known as "The Crab Effect," highlighting the self-centered, corrosive, and envious attitude of certain people within a group who feel threatened by people attempting to leave. Teenage friends in the secular world will often reach out their claws to pull back one of their escaping friends.

A young person who steps into church for the first time is 'changing buckets.' They are excited about their new life in Christ, but nervous. They crave relationships with people their age, but may not see many in the building. And if they see your youth group, they do not feel confident enough to walk over and introduce themselves. At this stage, they are vulnerable to The Crab Effect. You've seen it.

I've always been fascinated by the American Secret Service who protect current and previous presidents. They stand guard at major events wearing dark glasses while scanning the room, looking for people who are a potential threat. Train your youth team to take the Secret Service approach (without the dark glasses) to scan the congregation, looking for new young people to introduce themselves to. Let them know there is a new, more exciting and meaningful bucket to hop into!

Teach your youth how to reach out, engage, and build relationships with as many young people in the church as possible. They won't do it without practice. Train them and have them practice with one another. Make it fun. Building relationships is a Jesus-rooted ministry your youth and children need to embrace.

[39] *"And the second is like it: 'Love your neighbor as yourself.'* [b] [40] *All the Law and the Prophets hang on these two commandments"* (Matthew 22:37-40).

Any young person that is not connected to a young Christian group is vulnerable to leave. Don't leave them hanging by a thread, with one 'claw' in and one out of the church. Secure them into your youth bucket immediately.

Children are the most open generation for Christ. The success or decline of your future church depends on your willingness to invest and grow this next generation.

## EVANGELIZING CHILDREN: THE 4 TO 14 WINDOW

In 1990, Dr. Luis Bush launched the 10/40 Window ministry movement to reach nations positioned between 10 and 40 degrees north of the equator (Northern Africa, Middle East, and Asia). These nations encompass many of the world's least evangelized regions and have become a key focus of global mission efforts.

In 1992, Dr. Bryant Myers of World Vision, made a presentation titled 'The State of the World's Children: A Cultural Challenge to the Christian Mission. He presented survey results showing that nearly 85 percent of American Christians came to faith in Christ between the ages of 4 and 14.

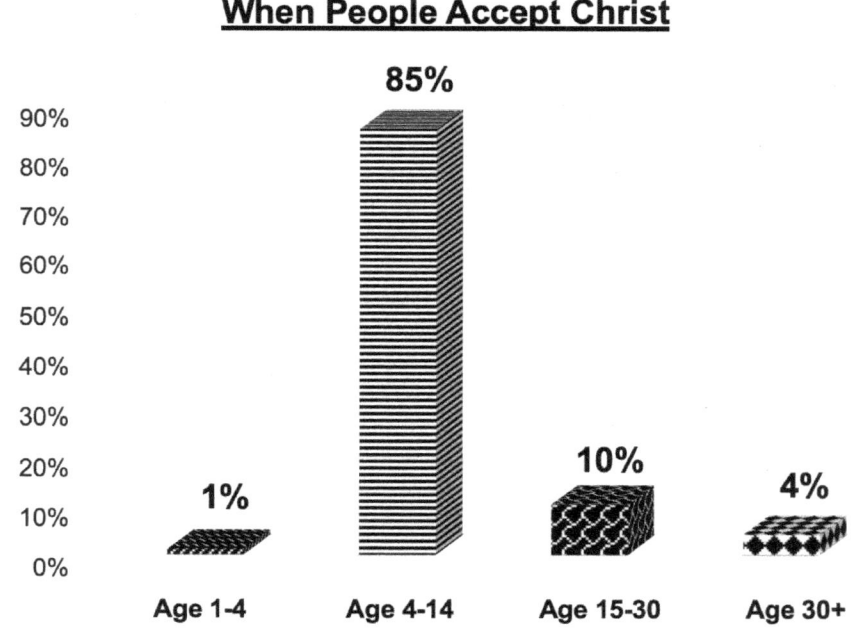

In 1996, Dr. Dan Brewster, Program Director for Compassion International, reviewed the survey and wrote an article titled: The 4/14 Window: Child Ministries and Mission Strategies." Dr. Bush noticed Brewster's article, and concluded that the key to reaching the least evangelized nations was through children, coining the phrase "The Window Within The Window." (The 4/14 Window within the 10/40 Window). In 2008, the 4 to 14 Window Movement was launched, headed by Dr. Bush and Rev. Nam-Soo Kim of the Promise Church in New Jersey. Soon afterward, the inaugural Global Summit took place, bringing together delegates from 65 nations, myself included. The Christian world opened its eyes to the unprecedented opportunity and urgency of impacting children for Jesus.

## CHILDREN RUN TO JESUS AND ADULTS RUN AWAY

Why do children accept Christ so easily? Is there a scientific or psychological reason? Are children in touch with their spirituality? Are they able to understand the Gospel at a young age? The answer is yes, yes, and yes!

To bring people to Jesus, they must be spiritually receptive and hungry; children naturally embody these qualities.

Kids across the world share common traits. The younger the child, the less influenced they are by culture or tradition. Children are naturally open to learning. Racism and prejudice are learned traits, almost unheard of with little children.

In 2018, my wife and I began ministering to leaders in Burundi, Africa. The story of Stanley and Livingstone is rooted there. In 1871, Stanley, a Welsh newspaper reporter for the New York Herald, was commissioned to find David Livingstone of the London Missionary Society. Livingstone, a missionary, served local Burundian tribes-people near Lake Tanganyika, the longest freshwater lake in the world.

People may label you a Livingstone if they find you so buried in office work that they question if you're still alive. David Livingstone was like that. His passion, aside from serving the native tribes, was to find the source of the Nile River. After 31 years, his supervisors considered him lost, since he never wrote (or emailed). That is until one day Stanley showed up and spoke those oft-repeated words "Dr. Livingstone, I presume?"

Hoping to haul back Livingstone, gain a big promotion, and perhaps ticker-tape parade, Stanley failed. Livingstone had no intention of returning. He had work to do... God's. Sadly, when Stanley returned with letters and documents from Livingstone, the Royal Geographical Society claimed he faked the letters by writing them himself. They had difficulty believing he found Livingstone among the jungles, rivers, and relatively unexplored areas of Africa.

Hand-writing experts eventually exonerated Stanley. He did, however, miss out on that parade.

Stanley's first impression of Africans was to judge them as "savages." Initially, he was cruel and demanding to those of the dark-skinned Wangwana tribe. Yet, with experience, he learned to respect them, writing he was "prepared to admit any black man...to a brotherhood with myself."[28]

Adults like Stanley may need life experience to change their views, but kids are different. Stanley required years of experience to shift his mind and see people through God's eyes. Kids? It's natural to them.

## KIDS: THE KEY TO ENDING RACISM

Our thinkSMALL teams in Burundi train local church teams to reach a mountain tribe named the Batwa. Batwa are the poorest tribe in the nation, and only 1 percent of the population. Batwa live in mountainous terrain, sleeping in grass huts.

---

[28] How I found Livingstone: travels, adventures and discoveries in Central Africa: including an account of four months' residence with Dr. Livingstone, Stanley, Henry M. (Henry Morton), 1841-1904, New York, Scribner, Armstrong & Co., 1872.

Their two greatest threats are fires that destroy their huts, and their lack of food. To feed themselves, they cut and sell grass to the nearby cattle-owners as feed. But they are most known for making pottery they carry long distances to nearby towns for sale.

Most people in Burundi belong to the Hutu or Tutsi tribe, at war for generations. Many of their leaders, however, agree on their desire to exterminate the Batwa.

Batwa pottery sellers walk from their mountain villages to town, greeted by townspeople shouting "Pigs! Pigs!" in the local language. Therefore, few people buy their wares.

The Batwa are illiterate, with no schools near their villages. They worship a nebulous God by burning sticks in their huts and wearing strings around their wrists. There is no Christian church in their communities.

In 2019, thinkSMALL Ministries' Burundian teams visited 6 Batwa villages to train children on staying safe from trafficking and drugs, and to bring them to Christ. Hundreds of Batwa adults and children gave their hearts to Jesus, and threw away their worship sticks and strings. The next step was to disciple the village, teach them God's Word, and raise children to become the first Batwa pastors.

There was only one problem; because the Batwa were illiterate, nobody could read the Bible. Due to their isolation, no child had ever attended school. But, if they had money for tuition, uniforms, and books they were willing to walk several miles through the mountains to get there! Churches in America donated the money and the first day of school was about to begin. The children were overwhelmed with excitement, looking sharp as they replaced their tattered brown tribal clothes with modern school attire. The village adults cheered as they began their long walk to school.

The problem occurred the moment they arrived. As they stared at the classroom windows they saw the curious eyes of the other students; Hutu eyes. Tutsi eyes. Fear set in. They remembered who they were; the 'pigs of Burundi!' How would the other students accept them? Would they be bullied or perhaps beaten?

The bell rang. A teacher rolled a soccer ball onto the playground, and children ran to play. Laughter soon filled the air as Hutu, Tutsi, and Batwa children chased after the ball together. It seems the ball doesn't care where you came from. As it turned out, neither did the children.

Hatred is a learned thing. Little children easily accept other children, despite their differences. As in Burundi, the solution to ending racism is less about convincing adults to end their hatred, but by providing the opportunities for children to build intimate friendships with one another over time. There is a good reason that Jesus instructs us to "be like a child."

## AGE MILESTONES

According to social behavioral scientists, children journey through mental and psychological developmental stages to arrive at the belief system that eventually guides their lives.

```
┌ ─ ─ ─ ─ ─ ─ ─ ─ ─ ─ ─ ─ ─ ─ ─ ─ ┐
│ Age 2: Worldview beginnings          │
│ Age 5: Greatest time of learning     │
│   Age 6: Moral values set for life   │
│     Age 12: Celebrate entering adulthood │
│       Age 13-14: Religion decided for life │
└ ─ ─ ─ ─ ─ ─ ─ ─ ─ ─ ─ ─ ─ ─ ─ ─ ┘
```

Age 2: Children begin developing their "worldview, beliefs or behavior."[29]

Age 5: Many scientists believe this is a child's optimum learning time. Five-year-old kids are like sponges, soaking up every bit of information. They have nonstop energy. They run around your house, make continual messes, sneak cookies, binge on sugar, and rarely finish healthy breakfasts. God grants a special blessing to parents of such children. Take heart. Due to their unbounded energy, they may someday rule your nation.

It seems a 5-year-old child's favorite question is, "Why?"

"Daddy, why are trees so big?"

"Because, son, they have great nutrition from the soil."

"Why?"

"Because son, the rain falls from the sky, lands on the ground, sinks into the roots, and gives them lots of good things so the tree will grow tall."

"Why?"

"Because God made it so."

"Why?"

---

[29]  Barna, George. Transforming Children into Spiritual Champions: Why Children Should Be Your Church's #1 Priority, page 53.

"Uh...ask your mother."

Kids are humble, hungry to learn. They certainly don't feel they have it all figured out! Educational pride? You've got to be kidding. Adults on the other hand? Well, I think you know the answer.

Children typically secure their moral foundations between ages six to nine. With little life experience, they depend on adults to shape their moral code.

Children understand kindness. They equate it to truth. A friendly adult, such as a well-meaning school teacher, can influence a child's moral belief system. In a child's mind, a kind adult would never lie or deceive. Trusting and believing an adult is easy. Children are vulnerable to deceptions, whether intentional or not, from friendly adults.

Parents and the local church are responsible for instilling a child's Christian moral belief system. Children attend primary school for approximately 8,000 hours. It is crucial to shield them from influences that appear harmless but may ultimately prevent them from living a life firmly rooted in Christ.

*"...for even Satan disguises himself as an angel of light. 15 Therefore it is not surprising if his servants also disguise themselves as servants of righteousness, whose end will be according to their deeds,"* (2 Corinthians 11:14-15).

By age eight, most children have established a worldview, a lens through which they interpret society, its morality and their role within it.

Age 8-12: Children become more independent, wanting to make decisions themselves.

Recently I spoke with a friend about his 10-year-old son. After I described the age milestones in this study, he laughed. "My 10-year-old son has returned to the "why" questions again! But instead of asking "Why are trees so big, he now asks me to justify everything I tell him to do."

"Son, go do your homework."

"Why?? I want to watch TV!"

"Son, go do your homework."

"Why can't I do it after the show?"

"Because I'm your Dad!"

"Why?"

"Watch out Son...You are skating on thin ice!"

*"Why can't they be like we were, perfect in every way? What's the matter with kids today?"*[30]

Age 13 or 14: A child's belief system or religion is likely in place by age 14, with an 85 percent chance it will never change. A young child's mind has a belief system like wet cement, easy to imprint. But if you wait too long it hardens to a point where a spiritual jackhammer is needed!

Barna Group conducted three years of research compatible with these findings. They learned that, "a majority of Americans make a lasting determination about the personal significance of Christ's death and resurrection by age 12."

According to Barna, our spiritual beliefs are hardened when we reach our early-teen years. They found that these beliefs typically are permanent. Their national poll of 13-year-olds and an equivalent study of adults showed identical belief profiles on a dozen major spiritual issues: The nature of God, Satan, the Bible, the afterlife, Jesus Christ's sanctity, how to obtain God's favor, and spiritual forces' influence on a person's life, were among those beliefs.

---

[30] Bye, Bird, Birdie, "Kids"

"In essence," the researcher said, "what you believe by 13 is what you will likely die believing."

The founder of the Barna Group, George Barna, states in his book, *Transforming Children into Spiritual Champions* "If people do not embrace Jesus Christ as their Savior before they reach their teenage years, the chance of their doing so at all is slim."

So when is the best age to share the Gospel with children? NOW!

## Keep In Mind:

1. Adults are most open to the Gospel during times of crisis.

2. Church youth teams play an essential role in helping new young church attenders forge strong relationships, safeguarding them from being pulled back into non-Christian peer groups.

3. Children are ready to receive Jesus but need parents and church to help them maintain their faith in the face of secular culture.

Thus far, you have read about the threats to the local church, and the importance of reaching and discipling the youngest generation. The challenge is that many churches reside in apathetic or resistant communities. Community residents or leaders may resist your well-intentioned plans to influence their children.

That's understandable.

Rather than pulling in your nets, rowing to shore, and putting your boat up for sale, realize there are ministry strategies even a resistant community can accept.

In the next chapter you will hear how strategic champions have utilized the Least Resistance Strategy to navigate their vessel into rugged harbors. Their stories will inspire you to identify your community's most open yet unmet entry points! Read on!

# PART 4

# BELOW THE SURFACE: JESUS AND OTHER LEADERS' LESSER-KNOWN SUCCESS STRATEGIES

A ship cannot float in shallow water. I wrote the first three parts of *Fishing For The Future* to ensure you had enough depth to lift you off the ocean floor. Now it's time to chart your course, push off from the dock, and sail on!

The following five chapters will guide you with customizable strategies to ensure that your church becomes younger, larger, and packed with more emerging young leaders!

## CHAPTER 10

# STRATEGIC CASTING: TRANSFORMING APATHETIC COMMUNITIES FOR CHRIST

---

[16] *"I am sending you out like sheep among wolves.*
*Therefore, be as shrewd as snakes and*
*as innocent as doves."*
—Matthew 10:16

---

"Avoid what is strong, and strike what is weak"
—Sun Tzu

---

How do you make your church a hero in a town that doesn't seem to care?

The Least Resistance Strategy has long been used in military, business, and ministry to overcome resistant forces. In this chapter, you will read examples of leaders who achieved greatness by applying this method. Reading these inspirational stories will stir your mind and prepare you for the final strategies that can make your church a hero—even in the most apathetic or resistant communities!

## MY DAY AS AMERICAN AMBASSADOR

I have always had a heart for business strategy. Prior to ministry I was an entrepreneur, later spending years as a national manager for a global food company. It made sense that when God called me to ministry in Thailand, I would serve in some form of business ministry. I began training churches to develop in-house businesses such as coffee shops or salons to support the church and reach people for Christ.

Eventually I interviewed with an international nonprofit organization to start their national micro-enterprise program in Thailand. Micro-enterprise is also known as 'business for the poor,' where financially underprivileged people are given small loans and assistance to build successful 'micro' businesses, such as street vendors. Micro-enterprise has become an enormous industry, existing in most nations today.

In 2006, I attended a global conference on micro-enterprise in Bangkok. I was excited to meet the man who created it, Dr. Muhammed Yunis.

Dr. Yunis is from Bangladesh. Years ago, he would walk along the city streets to his office at a local bank. Each day he would pass by poverty-stricken residents sitting on the sidewalk. Next to them lay rectangular-shaped cloth upon which home-made shoes, baskets, or snacks sat. One day he stopped one of these vendors and asked how they began in business. Broken hearted, the woman recited her story of how loan-sharks provided the start-up money but charged her 200 percent in interest. She, as others, were unable to repay their debts. They were destitute. He was stunned. And angry.

He returned days later and met with one of the loan sharks. He paid off her debt, but also loaned her money for a minimal interest rate she could afford. He did the same for the rest of the vendors on the street, launching the micro-enterprise industry.

It is important to note that Dr. Yunis chose to reloan the vendors the principal balance instead of relinquishing the entire debt. Some people may disagree with his strategy. But he had two goals; to set these people free from loan sharks, and to protect their dignity. Soon the vendors could pay off their loans, purchase future materials with the profits they made and become self-sufficient.

Bangladesh is one of the most poverty stricken nations in the world. The national government struggled for generations, attempting to fix this issue. Dr. Yunis' heart for the poor led him to expand his idea to thousands of others. While many street vendors prayed to make enough money to shoe their children's feet, he took them beyond.

In 1983, he began the Grameen Bank, designed for poor Bangladeshis. Some of these people became members of the board of directors, empowered to make decisions on maintaining the accounts and to provide additional loans. By 2007, the bank had 7.4 million borrowers!

Due to his efforts to relieve poverty, Dr. Muhammad Yunis was awarded the Nobel Peace Prize in 2006. Dr. Yunis, by the way, is not Christian, but Muslim.

Back to my story of the conference; My wife Paula and I wore our best clothes: I was in my best suit and Paula wore her most beautiful outfit. We were still the most underdressed people in the place.

The building was magnificent. The conference was extravagant, attended by delegates from around the world. Security was tight. The Thailand Prime Minister, national ambassadors, United Nations members, UNICEF, and at least 100 global organizations were there.

We were also running a bit late. Most of the crowd were registered and had received identification badges. In a rush, we paid little attention as they signed us in and gave us ours. I didn't notice the additional small badge they pinned on my suit.

For the next 45 minutes, people worked through the crowd to introduce themselves and engage us in conversation. I hit it off well with the French ambassador who insisted we soon get together for lunch. After hors d'oeuvres we were escorted to the front row in the auditorium. "Apparently," I whispered to Paula, "They heard about my success launching the coffee shop."

We were enjoying the speakers when Paula finally noticed. She laughed and pointed at the badge affixed to my suit. The registration desk mistakenly assumed I was the American ambassador! We had a choice. We could confess. Or we could just roll with it. We chose the latter (God forgive us). And I would do my best to represent my nation.

Soon we were whisked away on a private bus packed with 'other' dignitaries to an elaborate government building where the Prime Minister, 'other' ambassadors, and Dr. Yunis were to meet. Sipping some champagne and nibbling on (well, I'm not really sure what we were nibbling on), we shook hands and took private photos with Dr. Yunis and the Prime Minister. I've unsuccessfully attempted to feel guilty about this now for 20 years.

Why was Dr. Yunis' strategy so well received in Bangladesh? He set in motion a 'Least Resistance Strategy' that helped the local government solve a problem they had no answer to. And he became a national hero!

# SUN TZU

Sun Tzu's army was ruthless, but clever. Let's focus on the clever part.

Sun Tzu was a Chinese general during the Han dynasty around 544 BC. His approach to military engagement was to position his army to meet the enemy in its most vulnerable points, while minimizing the risk of his army.

He taught his soldiers how to equate water with a strategic victory. As water flows from the Chinese mountains, it follows the path of 'least resistance' increasing its momentum as it nears the ground. It converges into a power where, upon impact, becomes an unstoppable force.

Sun Tzu's willingness to apply this strategy established him as a military genius that modern generals still study.

## FRANCIS MARION

Francis Marion was known as the Swamp Fox. (How would you like that nickname?) He led an un-uniformed pack of horse-riding Americans that befuddled the British army in the Revolutionary War.

Marion was an officer in the Continental Army. Stationed in South Carolina, he fought using strategies unfamiliar to the British Army. Rather than face them head on with catastrophic results, he hid his horse soldiers in the forests waiting for the opposition army's march. When the aligned British forces were about halfway past, Marion would lead his riders out of the trees and attack them from the side. Like pesky flies, his army would attack and quickly retreat into the trees. His men were vastly outnumbered, yet very few died. But the enemy? They were devastated.

His most famous conflict was the Battle of Black Mingo, near Rhems, South Carolina. Marion's troops were, well, pesty. Attacking from the right and left of the exposed British Army, the redcoats in exasperation ran into a nearby swamp.

But that is not where the Swamp Fox got his name. That came from his strategy to 'out-fox' the British pursuers by cleverly maneuvering his riders through the American swamplands. After British Colonel Banastre Tarleton and his regiment pursued him through 26 miles of swamp he shouted "as for this damned old fox, the devil himself could not catch him!"

The ole' Swamp Fox was a vital contributor toward American independence by attacking the least resistant areas of the British force.

## BE LIKE MOSES (ROBERT, THAT IS)

Robert Moses once climbed a mountain and saw a bush burning with fire—oh, sorry, wrong Moses.

Robert Moses was born December 18, 1888. He became New York's greatest builder. There are "13 bridges, 416 miles of parkways, 658 playgrounds, and 150,000 housing units spending $150 billion in today's dollars" due to his ingenuity.[31] Although never elected to public office, he held 12 government titles; all simultaneously!

His most significant impact was from the mid-1920's to 1968. Moses' dream was to erect new buildings in the city he loved. But political obstacles stymied his attempts, causing him to change tactics. He discovered that the public was willing to support new parks development. His successful parks projects gained favor and leverage with the community. Soon the New York government and banks provided the funds to support other projects.

Moses was willing to adjust his original strategy to find openings that would eventually lead him to become the most successful builder in New York history!

Muhammed Yunis, Sun Tzu, Francis Marion, and Robert Moses were only a few of many who understood and applied the 'least resistance approach' to accomplishing their missions.

## FACING REALITY

A British businessman once boarded a direct flight from London to New York City. Settling in his first-class seat, all seemed well until he heard two bells on the intercom.

"Ladies and gentlemen, this is your captain speaking. As you know we just went through a bit of turbulence. Because of that experience, we seemed to have lost one of our engines. But don't worry. This airplane is an Airbus a380, fully equipped with 4 engines. Losing one engine is not a problem, but it will delay our arrival time in New York by 2 hours. Sit, relax, and we apologize for the delay."

A bit disturbed, but comprehending the situation, the businessman ordered another cocktail.

---

[31] The New York Sun, Robert Moses; https://www.nysun.com/article/arts-longing-for-robert-moses

As they continued their flight over the Atlantic Ocean, his short nap was interrupted by the sound of two more bells.

"Ladies and gentlemen, this is your captain speaking. Strangely enough, we seem to have lost another engine. But please do not be too alarmed. This airplane is an Airbus a380, fully capable of flying with two engines. I apologize, but it will delay our arrival time in New York by two additional hours. Sit, relax, enjoy another movie. And we apologize again for the delay."

You could now hear some tense murmuring from the passengers. The businessman became increasingly irritated. He worried he might miss his most crucial appointments. But one more cocktail seemed to calm his nerves.

Due to the alcohol and fatigue, he finally fell asleep. But 45 minutes later, the now all too familiar sound of two bells awakened him.

"Ladies and gentlemen, this is your captain speaking. I'm a bit embarrassed about this. It has never happened on this plane before but apparently we have lost another engine. But please do not panic. This airplane is an Airbus a380, fully capable of flying on a single engine."

That was all the businessman needed to hear! He stood up and shouted "This is ridiculous! If we lose that 4th engine, we'll be up here all day!!!"

## DETROIT

For a church in Detroit, Michigan, reality hit them hard. They knew the problem. They needed to get younger.

The pastor, staff, and elders held a meeting. It lasted ten hours. If there is a word to describe how the leaders felt about their church, it was Stuck. An elderly member who led the senior citizen ministry was the first to comment; "I don't want to go to my grave knowing my church will be close behind!"

They agreed to strengthen their commitment to empower the youth team, let them lead worship monthly and bring younger music into the church. Staff were unsure how the older crowd would accept the new music. They were likely more familiar with a Big Mac than a Toby Mac.

The youth team loved Jesus, but they complained that they were dealing with their own version of persecution from non-Christian youth antagonistic to their Christian faith. School friends were quick to remind them how out-of-touch they were with the rest of the people their age. It was painful.

The meeting began. By hour number four, all leaders agreed to a plan to empower the youth to reach non-believing kids into the community. The local townspeople were the problem. They had no issues with the church providing social services, such as food banks, hospital visits, and attending to the homeless. But kids? Keep your Christian evangelical hands off!

By hour number ten, the church had a plan. Kids in the low-income areas of their community were struggling. Schools were underperforming. Parents were uneasy. Many of the local children were fatherless, needing adult male influences. The local government, though concerned, was underfinanced and ill-equipped to respond effectively. And non-Christian organizations were concentrating their strategies elsewhere.

The youth team began to connect with children, volunteering their time to help with homework and guitar lessons. Some took kids to local baseball fields or the YMCA for basketball.

Soon every generation in the church joined in. Seniors became pseudo-grandparents, enlisting their life experience to offer children wise counsel and encouragement. Adult teams met with youth teams to listen, encourage, and support their efforts. The youth happily took leadership in maintaining and improving the ministry.

Some church members had expertise in tutoring or assisting children who felt neglected by absent fathers. They trained the youth team how to co-mentor these children successfully.

Another adult team presented the program to local community leaders. Teachers in low-income community elementary schools identified struggling students that needed mentoring and friendships.

An additional team conducted workshops on positive parenting, money-management, and guidance toward community resources, including food and housing support.

The community began to see the church in a new light, an answer to problems they could not adequately address! And there was a renewed spirit within the church.

Perhaps most meaningful, some neighborhood low-income families from the nearby neighborhood began attending with their children. Mothers, moved by the youth team's efforts, hoped their relationships with the children would continue.

Graduates of the adult workshops began coming to church. Some had been 'lapsed Christians,' with their belief restored through their class. Like prodigal children, they returned to His open arms.

The 'Reaching Out' program was a tremendous success. Giving the youth team greater responsibilities helped them develop the confidence to transition into young leaders and influencers. They strengthened their commitment to the church. They invited new friends. Some felt called to future ministry.

The church's reputation was transformed. It was no longer just a building on the corner. To the community, it became a crucial partner in making positive changes to the town.

## WINNING CHILDREN FOR JESUS IN A COMMUNIST NATION

In 2012, a major denomination in a communist nation invited us to launch our ministry in their country. Typically, that is not an issue. But this time, we were not sure. Evangelism outside of the church walls is illegal there. Caught and you could spend years in prison. Some never return.

Initially, I was unsure how our ministry could be successful in a nation so restricted. Our strategy is training church teams to evangelize and disciple children.

Never underestimate Christians who feel called to a mission. At the first meeting, I alternated between encouraging the team and expressing my concerns for their safety. Finally, I was interrupted by the team leader. "Pastor Gary. We are called to the same mission you are. We have already decided to see our nation discipled in Christ. That part is finished. Let's just brainstorm about how we are going to do it."

I could finally understand what Jesus meant when He said, "Never have I seen anyone...with such great faith" (Matthew 8:10). It made me question my own.

The Least Resistance Strategy went into motion. The government was feeling pressure from worried parents. Drug pushers had been addicting children with candy-flavored methamphetamine tablets. About 30 percent of primary school-aged kids were regular users. Others became drug 'mules' delivering pills given to them by drug pushers to children around the school.

Parents had been asking schools and government officials "How will you protect my child from these drugs?" Neither had an answer.

Since our ministry teams train churches to teach children to resist drugs, it was a perfect 'least resistance' opportunity. Eradicating the church was a government goal. But for today, ridding the nation of drugs was more urgent. Illicit drugs were damaging the economy—

addicted patients with little ability to pay for services filled local hospitals. Pushers and users packed prison cells. And nothing the government was doing would stem the tide. The police were stretched thin trying to control the drug problem while also fighting more violent crimes. The government's reputation was deteriorating day by day.

The thinkSMALL team secured an appointment with the government, offering to bring anti-drug outreaches to the communist sponsored schools. The government was initially skeptical about allowing a Christian organization in their schools. But the size of their problem surpassed the size of their anxiety. The team promised not to share Christianity to the children and the government quickly jumped on board, signing a contract with the Christian church allowing it to enter their schools. To our knowledge, this is the first communist/church school partnership contract in the history of this nation.

The drug-prevention outreaches were more than mere education. They were fun! Teachers and administrators loved them. So did the children. At the end of each outreach, the church emcee would ask the children if they would like to attend another. Overwhelmingly, they shout YES!!

The emcee then would point to a little building near the school with a cross on the door. "That's great, kids! On Saturday, we will have a different outreach inside that building. It will teach you how to resist trafficking. And it will be just as fun as the one today!"

On Saturday, the children from the school walk through the doors of the church. They learn how to be safe from traffickers. The outreach finishes with the Gospel. Typically, over 90 percent of the children pray to receive Christ and begin attending church. No law has been broken as there is no restriction to sharing the Gospel inside a church building.

Recently, we celebrated our 10th anniversary in this nation. Trainers have coached over 80,000 children on how to stay safe from drugs, trafficking, and abuse. And over 65,000 have come to Christ, with over 70 percent entered into discipleship.

When you find the path of 'least resistance,' everyone benefits. And the Kingdom grows.

Customization

[20] *"To the Jews I became like a Jew, to win the Jews. To those under the law I became like one under the law (though I myself am not under the law), so as to win those under the law"* (1 Corinthians 9:20).

Customize. Never compromise.

McDonald's began as a small hamburger joint in San Bernardino, California in 1940. Have you noticed how much it has grown? There are more than 40,000 McDonald's restaurants in the world. Approximately 2,000 stores open yearly, about one every four hours! If we could only get people as hungry for Jesus as they are for Big Macs!

McDonald's Corporation learned that although people love hamburgers, local preferences for spices, sauces, sizes, and cooking styles vary by nation. In Egypt, the Big Mac is bigger than ones in the USA, but less salty. Argentina cooks the burgers on coal rather than a grill. McDonalds in India doesn't serve beef but chicken in their "Maharajah Mac!" Order a 'Pickled Red Onion' burger on your next trip to Denmark. Purchase a Teriyaki burger in Japan. Big Mac sauces are sweeter or spicier depending on the flavor preferences of specific nations. It's still a Big Mac. But it has been customized to fit the customer.

What about pizza? It's perhaps the world's most popular food. Yet if you visit Bangkok, don't expect tomato sauce on your pizza. Coca Cola adds more or less sugar based on the taste preferences of young people in different countries.

You do not need to compromise your goal of bringing the Gospel to your community. But you need a bridge to the entry point where the apathetic or resistant community welcomes you.

As an 18th Century Tennessee hunter once said, "Never serve fried squirrel to the Queen of England."

## APATHETIC CONGREGATIONS

Have you noticed fewer people hanging on your every word at Sunday services? Does it seem like an ever-smaller group is participating in overt worship and prayer? Are congregants using smartphones in church focusing on something other than their Bible?

A recent survey asked Americans what they valued most in their lives. The top two answers were comfort and entertainment. How would your congregation respond to that survey?

Has the spirit of apathy made its way into your congregation? If so, you are not alone. Jesus knows how you feel.

[8] *"'These people honor me with their lips, but their hearts are far from me"* (Matthew 15:8).

How can you awaken your church to a new spirit of vitality? How do you stir up an apathetic congregation? (Hint: Don't shout at them).

One of the most effective ways to revitalize a congregation is to present a fresh vision with a credible strategy that meets the unmet needs of the community. Excited leaders with compelling visions, believable plans, and firm commitments are always listened to. It may be just what your church is waiting to hear!

### Keep in Mind:

1. The Least Resistance Strategy involves entering resistant or apathetic areas at their most vulnerable points.

2. In seeking opportunities, look for what locals are concerned about, build a plan and engage all age groups in your church.

3. Customize, but never compromise!

Jesus had a message for the world. But how was he going to get people to listen? Miracles have a way of getting people's attention, and so does social ministry. Jesus used social ministry to pry open people's hearts to deliver His salvation message.

In today's world, a carefully designed social ministry strategy may be your best choice in utilizing the Least Resistance Strategy. It is the optimum approach in reaching the most children in the shortest time for your church. Let's learn from the Master Fisherman!

# BAITING YOUR HOOK: REACHING CHILDREN THROUGH SOCIAL MINISTRY

*"It is my judgment, therefore, that we should not make it difficult for the Gentiles who are turning to God."*
—Acts 15:19

"If kids are so extraordinary, where did all the ordinary adults come from?" (anonymous)

## WASHINGTON STATE

Seattle, 1964. Hysteria. Despite the anguish of many parents and the tension of understaffed and overwhelmed police, a near riot broke out. It was not a political one, but one generated by four young British long-haired, suit and tie bearing, rock 'n roll musicians, the Beatles. Over 14,000 jam-packed fans (mostly screaming teenage girls ogling for a better look at their fantasy boyfriends) gyrated, and went wild. During the concert, a girl who somehow found a way to climb high above the stage, fell and landed in front of Ringo's drums. They played on. They were used to this kind of thing. Other girls scrambled to climb over each other to reach the stage and perhaps touch one of their heroes.

Who knows if the Beatles played well or not. No one could hear the music above the ear-piercing squeals. Fans waited for months, skipping school lunches to try to buy almost impossible-to-get tickets. Girls brought homemade cakes, with the dream of delivering them to the Fab Four on stage. Only smashed remnants under their shoes remained.

The concert lasted only 30 minutes. The Beatles rushed off the stage to hop in a Cadillac. But it was surrounded by fans. They eventually snuck inside an ambulance for a quick getaway, finishing their evening at the Edgewater Hotel in Seattle, overlooking the bay while holding fishing poles out their bedroom window with hopes of catching a salmon. True story.

In this chapter, we will look at one of the most essential keys to how Jesus 'caught' His fish--social ministry. Then we'll review how you can implement these strategies to reach community children's unmet needs to bring them into the Kingdom, and strengthen the future of your church!

## ISRAEL

[48] *"Unless you people see signs and wonders," Jesus told him, "you will never believe."* (John 4:48)

It's tough being a star.

To His fans in Capernaum, Jesus was a major event. Indeed, He knew how to draw a crowd. The house where Jesus was teaching overflowed into the street. Rather than screaming girls, spiritually hungry adults crowded each other to get a better look, and hear His teaching.

In the back of the crowd, four men were carrying their paralyzed friend on a mat. They were sure Jesus' touch would get him on his feet again. The problem was there was no way to get to Him. One of the men (who might have been a roofer) may have suggested hauling their comrade to the back of the home, raising him to the roof, carving a hole and dropping him down. There is nowhere in the scriptures where they asked permission from the owner. Yet somehow all four men agreed (which was perhaps one of the Bible's lesser-known miracles).

Like the girl who fell from the rafters in front of Ringo, the man dropped before Jesus.

I wish someone would have snapped a photo of Jesus' facial expression when a slow-motion body came down from above. (Mark 2:1-12).

There are many things we know about our Lord Jesus. One of them was that He never missed an opportunity. Looking at the paralyzed man He said, "Son, your sins are forgiven." (Mark 2: 5)

If I were the man on the mat I would have been confused. "Your sins are forgiven?" I would have responded inappropriately by saying "Thank you, Master. But that is not why I came. My real problem is, I CAN'T WALK!"

Jesus' intention was always to heal him. But there was an even greater opportunity presenting itself.

"Who can forgive sins, but God alone?" (Mark 2:7). To that question, Jesus must have smiled thinking, "I'm so glad you asked."

He informed the stunned crowd that He was the Son of God, given the authority to forgive sins and open the door to eternal life. And with the power of a simple sentence, "I tell you, get up, take your mat and go home," (Mark 2:11) the man was healed.    There is no consensus on a definition of social ministry. So for this book, I'll define it this way: works of mercy that may include providing food, clothing, shelter, education, protection, visitation, or justice for the oppressed.

## THE HISTORY OF SOCIAL MINISTRY

Social ministry has a long heritage in our Christian faith. Social ministry in churches covers a variety of services, including food distribution, healthcare, prison and hospital outreach, and care for the elderly. But the most monumental opportunity for church growth is social work on behalf of children.

In the Old Testament, God often spoke about standing for those under the boot of injustice.

*"Defend the weak and the fatherless; uphold the cause of the poor and oppressed"* (Psalm 82:3).

*"Speak up for those who cannot speak for themselves, for the rights of all who are destitute.*

*9 Speak up and judge fairly; defend the rights of the poor and needy"* (Proverbs 31:8-9).

First-century Christians willingly responded to the Old and New Testaments' mandates to serve the vulnerable and protect the innocent.

The Catholic Church's mercy missions initiated social ministry worldwide. Catholic and Protestant churches today send missionaries to all nations with the goal of providing resources, assistance and spiritual guidance for suffering people.

## JESUS AND SOCIAL MINISTRY

Jesus and His disciples left Jericho and spotted Bartimaeus (Mark 10:46-52, Luke 18:35-43) sitting on the side of the road. Bartimaeus had heard the tales of Jesus and screamed, "Jesus, Son of David, have mercy on me!"

I wonder how many times Jesus rolled His eyes at His followers. Here they went again, this time trying to quiet Bartimaeus. But to his credit, he kept calling out. Finally, Jesus asked, "What do you want me to do for you?"

"Rabbi, let me recover my sight!" Jesus praised his faith, healed him immediately and sent him on his way. It's possible he turned back around and followed Jesus, now that he could see where he was going (Luke 18:35-43).

This miracle, like many others, was more than just physical healing. It was a social ministry. And it was a doorway to exposing Jesus as Savior.

Jesus instructs His church to do social ministry.

35 *"For I was hungry, and you fed me. I was thirsty, and you gave me a drink. I was a stranger, and you invited me into your home. 36 I was naked, and you gave me clothing. I was sick, and you cared for me. I was in prison, and you visited me* (Matthew 25:35-36).

But He put it into perspective when he stated, 26 *"What good will it be for someone to gain the whole world, yet forfeit their soul? Or what can anyone give in exchange for their soul?"* (Matthew 16:26)

What good is it to feed, clothe, protect, care for, and visit people and yet not offer them the chance for eternal life?

Even non-Christian organizations care for people in need. But for Christians, social work is not the end, but the means. As important as it is, to a follower of Christ social work marks the start, not the finish.

## THE ULTIMATE PURPOSE

Lazurus eventually died. What occurred after his second death was a far greater miracle than the first.

Jesus used social ministry as a compassionate bridge to His salvation message. He used miracles to get people's attention. There was something more critical He wanted to say.

We all love to talk about Jesus' miracles. They fascinate us. They amazed his audience.

*12 "And the man jumped up, grabbed his mat, and walked out through the stunned onlookers. They were all amazed and praised God, exclaiming, "We've never seen anything like this before!"* (Mark 2:12)

Jesus' miracles were so dramatic many people thought he was merely a magician. If that was true, He had a terrible agent. Rather than 'perform' in the largest arenas, Jesus did most of His miracles with small audiences, often telling the recipient of His miracle not to tell anyone. Clearly, He wasn't in it for the money.

People often view social ministry and evangelism as independent from one another. But Jesus linked them together. John wrote that Jesus' miracles had a purpose that surpassed the physical world.

*Now Jesus performed many other things in the presence of the disciples, which are not written in this book; but these are written so that you may believe that Jesus is the Christ, the Son of God, and that by believing you may have life in his name* (John 20:30-31).

Raise a few people from the dead, heal some from paralysis, instantly transform a leper, change water into wine, and feed a few thousand people with a handful of fish and bread, and you will get their attention.

That is the point.

*"Believe me when I say that I am in the Father and the Father is in me; or at least believe on the evidence of the works themselves"* (John 14:11).

Jesus understood the eternal purpose of miracles. Without them, who would listen to His message? With them, they are all ears.

If you are a committed follower of Christ, you are instructed by the Most High to feed the hungry, visit the lonely and care for the sick (Matthew 25:35). But don't stop there.

Social ministry without the Gospel is incomplete.

## JESUS ULTIMATE PURPOSE AND OURS

Social ministry should always have an evangelical objective.

Dr. Dan Brewster wrote in 2005, "The poor and exploited tend to be much more receptive to the Gospel. There is no group of people today whose lives are more disrupted than those of children and youth."[32] The church must reach out to children living disadvantaged lives. It is easy to think of low-income neighborhoods as the prime locations for the church to serve. Yet children in any neighborhood are under the threat of drugs, crime, abuse, trafficking, or internet exploitation. Social media, secularism, sexual identification, and mixed cultural messages result in confused children.

The divorce rate in America hovers around 50 percent. Most divorced adults are parents. Children of absentee fathers need older individuals' mentorship, guidance, and friendship. Lonely boys and girls often feel disconnected or misunderstood by the remaining parent. Boys need an older boy or man to help them through difficult years. Girls need guidance from women or mature teenage girls who have 'been there.' Often, damaged kids need less of a psychologist than an older, wiser Christian friend who will simply listen and lead them to Christ. In every community, children are vulnerable to destructive

---

[32] Dan Brewster, The 4/14 Window; https://www.compassion.com/multimedia/the%20 4_14%20window.pdf

influences. Jesus used people's physical and psychological needs as a bridge to His Gospel. It can be your bridge as well.

"The crisis, chaos and upheaval in our society leads to opportunities. Don't waste a crisis" (David Kinnaman, CEO Barna Group).

## SOCIAL EVANGELICAL MINISTRY, UNMET FELT NEEDS AND THE GOSPEL

Taking the Gospel to a resistant community is like offering a movie ticket to a starving man.

If your community is apathetic, it's up to you to show them why your church is essential. Why should they want your help if they can get it from someone else? Your goal should be to offer them something that fits their needs, yet is unavailable without your church. Build a unique bridge so significant to their lives that they beg for you to cross! As Jesus did.

## THE UNMET FELT NEED

Unmet felt needs are unsatisfied anxieties that live beneath the surface of our consciousness. The government, police, friends, school authorities, counseling, or the internet can't fix them. They differ from spiritual needs. We meet them through human methods first (the bridge).

## PARENTS' ANXIETY

"The test of the morality of a society is what it does for its children" (Dietrich Bonhoeffer).

All parents worry about their kids. They hope they will make the right choices. They stress about their kids' friends. They are concerned about the things they cannot effectively monitor outside the home, such as social media, videos, or pornography. They worry they will not be the bully's victim, nor become one. I'm sure Adam and Eve had stressful discussions about their first two sons.

Sometimes this anxiety is buried beneath the surface. But it is there. And, in most cases, it is not being served. Every parent has a subconscious voice that speaks. "Will they be OK? Will they be safe? Will they be offered drugs? Will someone harm my child?" To worry is natural. But some worries cannot be solved by the government, the police, or school authorities.

*A mother who calls a police department and asks "What are you doing to protect my child?" will find their answer unsatisfactory.*

*"Ma'am, we will arrest the person who hurts your child."*

*"I don't care what you do to that person! I want my child safe from harm!"*

The police, the school, the local community center, improved street lighting, and sidewalks do not fully satisfy parental concerns when their child leaves for school. Schools can only ensure children's safety during school hours but cannot protect children before the first class, or after the final bell.

## WHAT TO DO

Begin with yourself and parents in your church. When you consider children in your community, what breaks your heart? Drugs? Abuse? Internet exploitation? Educational or health issues? Crime risk? Gangs? Whatever bothers you is likely shared by others.

Have your elders or parents from your congregation visit local PTAs or other similar groups. Encourage them to participate in discussions and ask prying questions to learn what parents care about yet are under-served by police, schools, hospitals or other organizations.

Make a written survey and mobilize your youth team to collect information from neighborhood parents. Parents will be inspired that the local church (yours) cares enough to ask about their deepest unmet concerns!

List parents' most common concerns, then remove those already addressed by other groups. What's left are unmet community needs your church can consider. It may feel a bit like panning for gold, but once you find the nugget it will be well worth the effort! You are raising the perceived value of your church and opening the door to relationships, salvation, and long-term growth!

Your final step is to compare these unmet felt needs with the capabilities of your church and build a plan.

In thinkSMALL Ministries, we discovered a common unmet felt need; the anxiety parents felt about the safety of their children. To address that need, church youth teams lead outreaches where they train kids how to recognize the signs of trafficking, drugs and internet exploitation before they become victims. They learn how to protect one another from harm and to report any dangerous activities by adults.

This approach has not only built a bridge between children and youth in the local church, but opened the door to 95 unreached people groups in 15 nations.

At the end of the outreach, or perhaps at a different location, the youth team shares the Gospel. Kids happily embrace Christ as the 'Eternal Protector of Body, Mind and Spirit.'

Child protection is merely one example of how you can utilize the unmet felt need strategy. Find an approach that best fits you and your local community. But to build your church for long-term success, make it about kids.

## SO WHO SHOULD DO IT?

In 2020, researchers surveyed large churches in the United States with congregations over 2,000. They asked 582 church leaders about the importance of social work. Survey leader Warren Bird stated, "Large churches are learning that community service in Jesus' name is often a way to win the hearts of a skeptical unbelieving public."[33]

Smaller churches have the same opportunities as megachurches. They often operate more independently, have smaller leadership teams, and can make quicker decisions.

Whether you have a church of 20 or 2,000, seek out the unmet felt needs in your community and link it to child evangelism.

Even the most resistant communities can welcome your church with the right ministry approach.

**KEEP IN MIND:**

1. Jesus used social ministry as a compassionate bridge to His Gospel.

2. Social ministry for children opens doors to multiple segments of your community.

3. Build strategies to meet the unmet felt needs (UFN) in your community.

It takes a team of well-prepared fisher-people to bring in the largest catch. In the next chapter, we will look at why youth are your best team to reach children for Christ, experience ministry success, and be prepared to lead your church into the future!

---

[33] Warren Bird, Warren Bird Megachurches Are Becoming More Diverse, Focused on Special Needs Ministries Survey; https://www.s4program.org/resources/us-megachurches-are-be-coming-more-diverse-focused-on-special-needs-ministries-survey

## CHAPTER 12

# LURING TOMORROW'S LEADERS: PREPARING YOUTH TO LEAD YOUR FUTURE CHURCH

12 *"Don't let anyone think less of you because you are young. Be an example to all believers in what you say, in the way you live, in your love, your faith, and your purity."*
—1 Timothy 4:12

"Failing to invest in youth reflects a lack of compassion and a colossal failure of common sense.'
—Coretta Scott King

## JESUS WENT YOUNG

When He began recruiting His team, Jesus had one requirement: They needed to be capable of turning the world 'upside down.' He planned to train them for three years and then task them to spread His message to the world. He wanted people who were visionaries, would commit to the mission, and had the faith and energy to get the ball rolling!

With this assignment, who would YOU have recruited? I would have sought out the most experienced, successful, highly educated ministry leaders possible. And, of course, they would be over 40 years old. Jesus? He enlisted three young fishermen, a few more with nondescript jobs, and one the entire group hated. What was He thinking??

Jesus, too, was young although He was likely the oldest on the team. He often referred to His disciples as 'little children' ( Matthew 11:25, Luke 10:21, John 13:33, John 21). I assume it was a compliment.

In First Century Israel, Jewish children completed their first stage of religious training by around age 13. A few disciples may have joined Him shortly after. No one knows for sure, but most scholars estimate that His disciples were between 13 and 29 years old, with John the youngest.

In this chapter, we will look at some of the inherent leadership qualities of teenagers, and why you may be underutilizing them in ministry. Then we will explore ways to mobilize them into ministries that fit their passion, allow them to experience success, and open the door to hear God's call to become your future leaders.

## SEX, DRUGS, ROCK 'N ROLL

In the 1960s, many teenagers and young adults threatened to 'turn the Western world upside down.' The streets of Berkeley, California were a colorful mix of briefcase-carrying business people weaving through long-haired, dope-smoking youth in torn jeans and psychedelic-colored t-shirts. They called themselves hippies. It was happening, man!

Young people around the nation heard about the movement and found any way possible to get west to Northern California. Walking, hitchhiking, arriving in multi-colored beaten down Volkswagens, they swarmed like bees to honey. Girls sold flowers on the streets to passers-by. Hippies who openly denounced capitalism begged business people for money. Some slept on the streets. Some pooled their money to rent tiny, cheap apartments, squeezing a dozen or more into a room. A counter-culture emerged overnight, characterized by tie-dyed clothing, flower girls, free sex, drugs, and psychedelic music. Artists such as Janis Joplin, The Jefferson Airplane, Iron Butterfly, and the Electric Prunes performed protest songs against Western World trends promoting love, truth, and 'dropping out' of traditional society.

What stirred all this? The young generation watched a world in peril on television and hungered for change. They often tend to view man-made institutions as corrupt and selfish. So did Jesus.

Some young people protested in the streets. Others dropped out. Still others pivoted and launched a new way to protest the status quo; The Jesus Revolution was born. The collective force of this movement and the charismatic movement spread to most regions in the world. Young people led the way.

## WHY YOUTH ARE YOUR BEST TEAM

I am convinced that youth are the best candidates for new leadership roles in the modern church. They are actively looking to find meaning, purpose, and the assurance of God's approval. They are your church visionaries, and are passionate about social issues. They have available time. And they are hungry.

## YOUTH: HUNGRY FOR INDEPENDENCE

Since Adam and Eve, exasperated mothers and fathers have struggled to control their teenage children. It's good to know that it's a normal part of life.

In the 40s kids rebelled against parents by staying out late, drinking cheap alcohol, and smoking cigarettes. In the 50s they raced cars down main street and, to the chagrin of their parents, introduced Rock n Roll to the world. Eventually Rap, Hip Hop, Punk, Pop and Indie music would identify each new generation. What's next? God only knows.

In 1942, Billie Holiday introduced her hit song "God Bless The Child."

*"Mama may have, Papa may have…But God bless the child that's got his own."*

Throughout history, one undeniable fact remains; The youth want their own.

Teens share a lot in common. Here are two of them:

1. They seek independence.
2. They lean on each other.

Most young people perceive the world as a mess, blame the adults, and believe they can do better. You did too.

The more young people are encouraged and empowered to change the world, the more they will become who God created them to be. They are the dreamers, looking for ways to remedy the issues that plague their communities. At least they want to try.

## YOUTH: HUNGRY TO BE HEARD

Jimi Hendrix was one of the great musicians and influencers of youth in the 1960s. In 1969, Hendrix played an electric guitar rock-version of the "Star-Spangled Banner" at the Woodstock Music and Art Festival. It was loud, an electrifying blend of raw energy, soul and distorted tones. Intricate riffs and ear shrieking feedback blasted out of oversized speakers. Guitar notes wailed and screamed with immersive intensity. It was rough. It hurt the ears. Young people loved it. So did I!

In 1971, my senior year high school government class was divided equally between straight-arrow students, hippies, and druggies. I was a scholar athlete. The closest I came to using hard drugs was adding an extra dose of my daily vitamin C. But deep down, I fantasized being a hippie. Don't tell my mother.

Mr. Metcalf had the unfortunate assignment of teaching this eclectic group. He was the prototypical Christian of the day; conservative, well dressed and friendly. He was also a senator in the Washington State legislature. Mr. Metcalf struggled to understand today's youth, particularly those upset by the country's sociological, economic, and political difficulties.

It was a challenging year in the United States. The Vietnam War was in full force, the first war to have live broadcasts at battle scenes. It was the final year of the draft. Many young people were frightened that they might be sent to war. Every day, protesters marched down main streets and university campuses. They saw innocent people die, and blamed the adult generation. (Actually, they had a point). Young people felt rejected, unheard, and disrespected by those in power who were fueling the conflict. Most demonstrators were peaceful. Some threw rocks. Others burned buildings. Take heart. Many of these young people are now your political, business, and religious leaders. Their parents remain shocked even now.

Me? After high school I joined the Air Force.

Back to my high school story. While in Mr Metcalf's class, I had what I considered a stroke of genius. One of my best friends, Dave, was a brilliant rock guitarist. I thought he would be the ideal therapist to help Mr Metcalf better understand the psychology of his more edgy students. I convinced him to let Dave perform Jimi Hendrix's version of the "Star Spangled Banner" for the class in a small school theater down the hallway. Dave's instructions were to play it loud, and play it proud! It shook the building. Nearby classrooms emptied while kids crowded near the theater door. As the song finished, hundreds of students cheered while Mr Metcalf made it back to class on wobbly knees and deaf ears.

We took our seats and waited for his reaction. "Well, that was interesting. I'm wondering, though, why your music needs to be so loud."

I shouted, "It's the only way we can get you adults to listen!" The room fell silent. I thought I was dead. We all watched as the wheels churned in his head. After 15 seconds of silence, he spoke. "That makes sense."

Whew. Youth need to be heard.

## YOUTH: HUNGRY FOR A CAUSE

Youth are driven by social causes, particularly those that they perceive adults undervalue. Today's most discussed issues will likely change. But young people's desire to collaborate and solve problems will remain.

Unity toward solving an emotional cause inspires them, enhances their sense of security, confidence, and identity. Youth collaborate more easily than adults with varying agendas, motives, and time commitments.

Teens believe their lives are unique from adults who have gone before them. In their world, they 'get' each other. They lean on each other. They become formidable when they rally around a cause that shakes their soul.

## THE ARAB SPRING

For thousands of years young people have led movements that altered nations worldwide.

On December 17, 2010 a young Tunisian fruit vendor set himself ablaze to protest police harassment in his nation. Tunisian youth quickly rallied in his support, filling the streets to march against the national government. Soon, Arab youth in nearby nations rose in solidarity and rebelled in their own countries. The Arab Spring was born.

Multiple issues sparked the protests, including political corruption, acute poverty, unemployment, economic recession, and a sizable population of educated yet discontented youth.

From Cairo, the world watched thousands of young Egyptians rally against their government in Tahrir Square. Military tanks entered the crowd with soldiers refusing to turn their weapons upon the protestors. Globally, young people unified in support of their Egyptian peers, sharing live videos and inspirational messages on social media.

Facebook and Twitter were essential platforms for Tunisian and Egyptian demonstrators. A poll found that nine out of ten used Facebook to coordinate protests and raise awareness. They shared information about local protests through texts, emails, and blogs. Egyptian Facebook users posted clips of suspected crimes against protestors. Western youth, in particular, spread these stories to gain additional backing for the cause.

To Generation Z, the government's heavy-handed treatment of demonstrators was an attack on free expression and was untenable. Most young people outside the Arab world did not entirely grasp the political or economic reasons behind the protests. It didn't matter. They were witnessing an assault on their generation firsthand. It became a case of "us" (the youth) vs. "them" (the tyrannical adults).

Over the next year, youth from 12 other Arab nations took to the streets. Many of them lost their lives. But one thing is clear; When young people unite around a cause that impacts their generation, they can shake the world!

How do you find a ministry your youth can rally around? Your best opportunity is in cause-driven ministries that affect young generations and open the door to the Gospel.

Drugs and alcohol, cyberbullying, online exploitation, abuse, sexual identity, racism, academic struggles, hunger, gang violence, rampant sexual activity, and obesity are just some of the challenges existing in today's world. Christian youth agonize over these issues but feel powerless in doing much about them.

Young people are eager for a cause they can commit to, which resonates with their generation. They may look elsewhere if they can't find it in the church. Thousands of young people exit church each year to join non-Christian charitable organizations such as the Peace Corps. Others join Christian nonprofit groups that address social issues domestically or worldwide. Despite their 'good works,' few incorporate evangelism in their efforts.

Christian youth, however, realize that the underlying cause of their generation's social problems is spiritual[34]. They dream of their peers making decisions to follow Christ.

In most churches, youth are the most available yet least utilized group. They are creative. They have energy. They are socially conscious. They are hungry to make a difference. And they are available. They will make time for something they can lead and impact the world, even if the world is the community just outside your door. They are ready to lead.

---

34 Mark 7-21-23; [21]"For it is from within, out of a person's heart, that evil thoughts come—sexual immorality, theft, murder, [22] adultery, greed, malice, deceit, lewdness, envy, slander, arrogance and folly. [23] All these evils come from inside and defile a person."

## YOUTH: HUNGRY TO LEAD

Since the 1930s, adults have tried to dissuade teenagers from smoking marijuana. In 1936, Hollywood produced a movie called "Tell Your Children" (later changed to "Reefer Madness"). The film aimed to persuade parents to keep their children from marijuana. The movie begins with a high school principal talking with mothers and fathers. He warns them that marijuana causes schizophrenia, delusions, or worse. Later in the film, a teenaged marijuana smoker drives a car erratically, killing a pedestrian. His friend, also high on marijuana has a delusion that causes him to murder the driver's girlfriend. There's a trial, a suicide, and an eventual ending where one of the key players is sent to an asylum for the criminally insane! Now that is a story!

The movie soon became popular with teens as a comedy. Today it is a cult classic. Did it stop teens from smoking marijuana? Not one bit.

In the 1960's, the adults tried again. This time the target was cigarettes. Anti-smoking advocates spent millions of dollars on television advertising to scare children from 'lighting up.'

Health advocates produced television ads and school videos of cancer ridden people in hospital beds. Videos featured family members weeping at funerals for their deceased.

In 1965, the federal government decided to crack down against cigarette smoking by teenagers. Cigarette packaging was stamped with warnings relating smoking to lung cancer, heart and pulmonary diseases. In classrooms, teachers presented images of blackened lungs and videos of doctors warning teens not to smoke.

Highway billboards proclaimed words and images with messages such as "Smoking will kill you," "Smoking will turn your teeth yellow," and "Smoking will make you look like an animal" (depicting a smoking camel). Kids just laughed.

Despite the videos, education programs, television advertising, billboards, and print media, teenage smoking rates saw little change.

The problem was that these campaigns failed to address these two central questions: Why do teens smoke and why don't they quit?

Children and teenagers begin smoking for one or more of the following three reasons:

1. To be accepted by their peers (i.e. peer pressure)
2. To satisfy their desire for independence
3. To rebel against the adult generation.

'Liking the taste' is not on the list.

When asked why they don't quit despite health warnings, many teens refuse to believe they will become sick. Others state that life is so hopeless they anticipate dying young from war, poverty, or climate change.

Tina Rosenburg's book *Join the Club* details how a court case spurred teens to take the lead in the anti-smoking industry, succeeding where adults had failed.

In 1998, the four largest U.S. tobacco companies were found guilty of intentionally increasing nicotine in their cigarettes to addict smokers. They agreed to pay over $206 billion a year for 25 years. But they stayed in business.

They also agreed to release their internal documents. The public found out they had lied about being unaware that their products were causing cancer. They had also lied when they claimed not marketing cigarettes directly to teens. R.J. Reynolds, the manufacturer of Camel cigarettes stated: "To ensure increased and longer-term growth for the Camel Filter, the brand must increase its share penetration among the 14–24 age group which have a new set of more liberal values and represent tomorrow's cigarette business."

Not only was the cat out of the bag, but it was also eager to turn around and scratch those who had placed it there in the first place. When teens discovered that the adults running the tobacco companies were lying and exploiting their generation for personal profit, everything changed. It became a game of us against them—the youth pushing back against those who declared a type of war against them.

More than 600 teens attended the first Florida Teen Tobacco Summit in 1998. They raged against the adult-led tobacco companies who, they felt, were attacking their generation. And they made a plan, a truth campaign to expose the lies.

"We wanted to go more with a 'this is the truth' campaign," said Jared Perez, 17, a Palm Harbor University High School junior. "We want to show teens what the cigarette companies are doing. Smoking has the illusion of making you look like a rebel, but the truth is teen smokers are doing exactly what the tobacco companies want."

The teens capitalized on mobilizing kids to exert peer pressure rather than rely on anti-smoking health advertising.

With government support, teenage leaders created and starred in TV commercials, doing things that adults in the media wouldn't attempt, such as making prank calls to top tobacco company executives. Rosenburg writes: "Another ad showed a girl calling Lucky Strike's advertising account coordinator. "What is the 'lucky' part about Lucky Strike cigarettes?" she asks. "I really have no idea," the executive answers testily. The girl: "I mean, is it because . . . I might live?" After the ad executive hangs up on her, you can hear a group of girls laughing. In another commercial, Perez and another teen call an ad agency that advertises cigarettes. They offer the hapless person on the line an award for killing more teens than anyone else. Ad after ad showed teenagers getting people from the tobacco-industrial complex on the phone—and then torturing them. It is likely that never before in the history of public health had anyone done a media campaign based on prank phone calls."

As Peter Mitchell (the overseer of the 'truth' campaign) said: "No one likes to be manipulated. What do teenagers want? They are shopping for a way to rebel against their parents. Well, these people are even less cool than your parents."

Youth smoking in Florida, for the first time, declined. The students created a nonprofit organization, SWAT (Students Working Against Tobacco). It is still active today.        "Teenagers want to do what everyone else is doing and call it rebellion" (Tina Rosenberg).

## TOO YOUNG TO LEAD?

7 *"But the Lord said to me, "Do not say, 'I am too young.' You must go to everyone I send you to and say whatever I command you"* (Jeremiah 1:7).

"You are never too young to lead and never too old to learn" (Kofi Annan, U.N. Secretary-General 1997-2006).

"Has anybody seen my church's future? I swear it was here somewhere!" Most pastors claim it's becoming harder to find future leaders even though a majority believes "their church is doing what it takes."[35].

I disagree. If a church does what it takes, they will succeed. But to realize success, it 'takes' a strategy that fits today's youth. What worked yesterday falls flat today.

## THINK LIKE A FISH

I loved sitting in a rowboat with my father on an early Saturday morning, our lines in the water waiting for the fish to bite. I remember

---

[35] Barna Group, The Aging of America's Pastors; https://www.barna.com/research/aging-americas-pastors/

one day watching in frustration as my dad reeled in four trout before I had a single tug on my line!

Finally, I blurted out, "This is unfair! Why do YOU get all the fish?"

"Gary," he said, "To catch a fish you need to think like one."

He then lifted his pole from the water. On his hook were little red salmon eggs, while on mine was a worm. I had the proper technique, a good fishing rod, and a sharp hook. I also had the wrong bait. Apparently, the fish in this lake grew tired of eating earthworms. Can you blame them?

To catch today's youth, don't use yesterday's fishing strategies. Learn to think like a fish!

## CHANGE YOUR BAIT!

Yesterday's bait will not attract today's youth to ministry. Look to harness young people's passion for social issues, enabling them to lead ministries that address these problems and bring others to Christ.

Earlier in this chapter, we reviewed key attributes of today's youth. They are overwhelmed with news about worldly problems. They (correctly) blame adults for causing them. They believe they are the generation capable of solving these problems. They bond quickly, support one another, and prioritize their generation above all others.

The difference between secular and church youth is that Christian youth believe Jesus is the ultimate answer to all problems.

One of the best ways to develop future leaders is by allowing them to lead and succeed in a ministry that impacts their generation, stirs them emotionally, and brings people to Christ.

## MOBILIZE YOUR ARMY

[13] *Suddenly, a prophet approached Ahab, king of Israel, saying, "Thus says the Lord: 'Have you seen all this great multitude? Behold, I will deliver it into your hand today, and you shall know that I am the Lord.'"*

[14] *So Ahab said, "By whom?"*

*And he said, "Thus says the Lord: 'By the young leaders of the provinces.'"*

*Then he said, "Who will set the battle in order?"*

*And he answered, "You."'" (1 Kings 20:13-14)*

And Ahab answered sarcastically, "Wow. Thanks a lot."

You are the one who must prepare your young army for victory.

## CALLING

Most pastors claim God called them to ministry in their teenage years. Today's youth are ready for the same call. But it will not likely happen without you creating an environment where it can occur.

Most young Christians are 'hooked on Jesus' but unsure of their future. Despite how they portray themselves to the world, they struggle with doubts. Teachers, parents, friends, and the media all compete to influence their choices. This myriad of voices filling their heads makes it difficult to discern who is Who. No wonder it is often difficult to hear God's voice.

Many young people are open to church leadership but feel ill-equipped. They don't want to fail, let you down, or disappoint God. Mostly, they don't feel called.

The world's distractions and their insecurities create a form of spiritual ear wax. God may be calling, but they do not hear the phone. Young people often best hear God's confirming voice when leading another person to Christ.

## SUCCESS

Most people struggle with doubt, youth in particular. They most often hear the call to ministry while in the process of success.

Few professional baseball players felt 'called' to the sport before they picked up a ball and threw their first strike or got their first base hit. Golf is a difficult and frustrating game until you finally hit your first lucky drive down the middle of the fairway. Suddenly you sense a near-silent voice whispering "You can DO this!" Success breeds confidence, rather than the other way around. And success in ministry increases the opportunity to hear God's 'you can do this' voice!

When young people succeed, they hear God's voice more clearly. Self-doubts are replaced with self-assurance. A vision is stirred and the earwax that previously blocked their ability to hear His call to ministry begins to melt away.

My wife Paula recently told me a story of her first time fishing with her family in West Texas. She was six years old. She sat in the boat, relatively bored with the whole scene, wishing she was back on shore to play with her friends. A moment later, she felt something pulling on her line! A few minutes later, she showed off her prized catch: a four-inch baby trout! To Paula, it was a marlin! She bounced and squealed excitedly, shouting "I can do it! I can do it! I can do it!"

She could not wait to get her fishing rod reloaded, worm attached and plunked back into the water! As French novelist and playwright Alexandre Dumas once proclaimed: Nothing succeeds like success.

Creating an environment where young people will experience ministry success prepares them for future achievements. It's a springboard, building momentum and energy that propels them to reach even greater heights.

Ministry failure, however, steals energy, lowers confidence, and kills future motivation.

To cultivate future leaders, engage them in life-changing ministries where they can experience the joys of success! Create opportunities for them to build a collection of successful memories, reinforcing their belief God will use them in ministry. And when He eventually calls, they will run to pick up the phone and shout "YES!"

## SOCIAL EVANGELICAL MINISTRY (SEM)

Planting trees or cleaning the trash from city streets will not inspire young people to pastoral leadership. They need a social ministry with an evangelistic goal (SEM).

Gather your youth leaders. Share your vision. Help them develop a ministry that turns them on and addresses a community need that targets their generation or younger. Most importantly...

## LET THEM LEAD

Young people will not envision themselves as future church leaders if they are prohibited from leading at a young age! Let them take the reins. Youth need to believe that their success results from their own efforts.

Your role is to mentor, not to manage. Empower, don't restrict. Open the gate and let the horses run! Encourage them to succeed but help them recognize the benefit of failure..

"... *suffering produces perseverance; 4 perseverance, character; and character, hope* (Romans 5:3).

A ministry that combines addressing youth social problems with evangelism will strengthen your church and raise new leaders.

## WHY MOBILIZE YOUTH TO KIDS

I'm convinced the quickest way to impact your church's future is by engaging youth in social ministry for children. Most pastors assume youth want nothing to do with their younger brothers and sisters. That is a mistake. Youth just need a big enough reason.

Here is the biggest reason; **To redeem the world for Jesus.** Satan has one goal, to exterminate Christianity. His primary strategy to accomplish his mission is to prevent children from knowing Jesus. He has declared war on their souls. And he is winning.

Satan has deceptively infiltrated the world's political, religious, entertainment, and educational arenas, promising freedom but delivering slavery.

34 *"Jesus replied, "Very truly I tell you, everyone who sins is a slave to sin"* (John 8:34)

23 *"For the wages of sin is death, but the free gift of God is eternal life through Christ Jesus our Lord"* (Romans 6:23).

Satan uses the 'Least Resistance Strategy' by reaching the generation most open to his lies: the children. He aims to amputate the future of the church and thereby end the faith. Christian youth should arm themselves with the Word of God to carry out evangelistic ministries that destroy his ambitions.

Youth are visionaries and driven by causes. There is no higher cause than winning the world for Christ. The most effective way to achieve this goal is to reach, empower, and mobilize the generation Satan fears most: children.

In Chapter 7, we discussed Asaph's writing in Psalms 78:4-8. His vision was to see his broken nation return to God. Asaph encouraged God's people to evangelize and disciple two generations of children to become Israel's transformational leaders. Religious and political leaders have successfully applied his strategy for more than 3,000 years. It's time for the local church to embrace this strategy to return our communities to Christ!

In Asaph's perspective, two generations would span over 40 years, enough time to raise a child for God, allow them time to parent a second generation, and raise them to become transformational leaders.. In today's world, 'two generations' are youth and children.

Unleashing the energy of these two groups can generate an unstoppable force to restore and rebuild any nation.

## MIDDLE SCHOOL TRIALS

Middle school is a danger zone for children. Peer pressure, sexual temptations, puberty, and an increased quest for independence may prompt kids to make destructive decisions. Who is going to mentor them? Who will guide them through the middle school gauntlet? To the children, youth are the ones they look to most. They are their heroes.

Christian youth need to step into this battle. Is it possible you have not emphasized this enough?

Set a goal to establish a youth-led ministry that can benefit children socially, protect them from evil, and foster positive relationships. Consider community needs that involve child education (such as tutoring), drug prevention, safe social media activities, and resisting trafficking, and exploitation. Youth can provide training and environments where children can develop new Christian friends.

Whatever social ministry your youth choose to lead, make sure its ultimate goal is evangelism, keeping in mind that children are the most open to the Gospel!

*Let each generation tell its children of your mighty acts;* (Psalms 145:4-7).

**KEEP IN MIND:**

1. Empower Youth Leadership: Like Jesus, recognize the potential in young people and their ability to lead.

2. Focus on Cause-Driven Evangelical Ministries: Mobilize youth to lead ministries for young people, experience success and hear God's voice for leadership.

3. Youth Evangelism and Mentorship: Emphasize the importance of youth evangelism and mentoring children, implementing a two-generation approach for long-term church impact.

Choosing the finest leadership crew is just the beginning of the voyage. A ship captain needs an admiral to help them reach their destination. In the next chapter, we will explore four key steps Jesus used to lead His young team. By implementing these steps, you will enable your team to achieve superior results and lead them into future leadership roles. Let's sail!

## CHAPTER 13

# TRAINING LIKE THE ADMIRAL: JESUS' 4-STEP PROCESS FOR YOUTH TEAMS (T.E.A.M.)

---

*40 "The student is not above the teacher, but everyone who is fully trained will be like their teacher."*
—Luke 6:40

---

It's easier to run with 100, than to drag 1
—anonymous

---

It was a tough start. Tampa Bay's NFL football team was terrible. After the team lost their 26th consecutive game, head coach John McKay was asked by reporters how he felt about his team's execution. He paused momentarily and answered, "I'm in favor of it!"

If you have ever felt that way, do not tell your staff!

It is easy to start a team, and much harder to make it successful. Jesus did it better than anyone. And the world was reborn.

In this chapter, we will outline some of the lesser-known ways that Jesus equipped His team to become the world's most successful Christian leadership team in the world: a four-step process called T.E.A.M.

## A MAJOR MIRACLE FOR THE MINERS

They cried for help. No one heard.

The ground shook with the destructive force of an earthquake. 2,257 feet below the surface 33 men felt the power and weight of falling earth. Death seemed likely, perhaps inevitable. With nowhere to go, they leaned on each other. They leaned on God.

The town of Copiapó, Chile lies 500 miles north of Santiago, resting in a lush green and blue valley of grapes, olives, tomatoes, avocados, and citrus. It is rich in history, with traces of human remains estimated from as long ago as 10,000 years. The Inca Empire ruled into the 16th century until Spanish explorers discovered it in 1742.

Copiapó's primary industry is mining copper ore and gold. Chilean miners have supported their families for generations. But on August 5, 2010, it all came crashing down.

Smoke and dust shot out of the ground like cannons. In mere seconds, the shaking stopped. But the fear had just begun. Miners below rushed to where they were expecting escape ladders. There were none, having never been installed.

Families rushed to the site in terror. Workers above ground stood shocked, seemingly paralyzed. Maybe they hoped it was an illusion, but reality slowly crept in. It was real.

With little food, water, or oxygen below ground, there was no time to waste. Rescuers quickly gathered and planned desperate strategies.

Below, the 33 miners gathered in prayer. They formed survival teams. They were unaware of how long they would need to wait for rescue. They did not know if it would be possible. But they knew they had to do whatever they could to survive.

They separated into small groups to ration food and water. Other teams encouraged and prayed. They sang songs, told stories and jokes to keep up morale.

Not knowing what was happening above ground, they leaned on prayer, encouragement, and planning.

Geologists, engineers, and rescue teams worked together. They eventually drilled a small hole to communicate with the miners and deliver water and supplies.

Unbelievably, 68 days passed without a breakthrough. Oxygen was dissipating. Straining their ears, they could sometimes hear the distant sounds of drills and voices calling to them. The prayers of millions around the world strengthened them.

On day 69, a ray of sun broke through the once-impenetrable roof. God had answered their prayers! Miners strained to hear the distant sound of cheers from above ground. A rescue capsule, the Phoenix, gently lowered to their underground camp picking them up one by one and into the grateful arms of their families.

Teamwork, encouragement, commitment, and prayer, above ground and below, overcame what was first considered impossible odds.

The power of prayer, encouragement, and planning can be an indestructible force. Just ask Jesus. His team changed the world.

Every successful ministry team must know its primary leader. Christian teams will follow the leader who openly follows Christ. By surrendering full authority to Him, He will take charge and provide the path to success.

8 *"Don't let anyone call you 'Rabbi,' for you have only one teacher, and all of you are equal as brothers and sisters"* (Matthew 23:8).

## THE JESUS-ROOTED TEAM LEADER

Jesus chose His leaders carefully. That is why perhaps like you, I was amazed when first reading how Jesus selected the denier-in-chief Peter to be the 'rock' of His church (Matthew 16:18). Under pressure, Peter denied even knowing Him (Matthew 26:69-74).

If you were Jesus, how would you respond? Would you offer Peter a promotion? Or would you dump him immediately?

Jesus saw something in Peter that I might have missed. Peter likely re-qualified himself for leadership that famous day on the beach. Immediately after breakfast, Jesus took Peter aside and asked him three times if He loved Him. Peter must have been waiting for this moment. He knew the boss was about to call him out. He may have suspected that this would result in his firing or demotion. Had three years of intimate friendship with the Son of God been destroyed by the fears and panic of one hour?

As Peter answered Jesus' questions, perhaps the Lord saw something in him. Jesus had long prepared Peter for a leadership role. Maybe the only thing Peter lacked was humility. As Jesus looked into the eyes of Peter that day, He saw a humble, sorrowful man. A humbled version of a confident Peter was one who Jesus could anoint for as a leader. Peter was humiliated, but it impacted him in such a way that Jesus assigned him the most crucial role of the church. And Peter never lost his gratitude, love, and loyalty for the one who forgave and empowered him.

Gratitude can lead to loyalty and love. I've often said my greatest motivation to serve the Lord is my gratitude. He saved me despite my rebellious youth, selfish choices, and pain I caused others. Nothing I can do will measure the salvation and life He has given me. Gratitude is a motivator.

When choosing a team leader, look for someone passionate about the vision, who exhibits confidence, but is humble in spirit. That person will be grateful and highly motivated to lead humbly. They will become an influencer for others on the team.

"When you understand that leadership is influence instead of position, that changes everything" (John Maxwell).

A team leader's primary responsibility is to foster belief in the team's vision, celebrate success, clarify goals and motivate them into action.

## WHAT ABOUT ROLES?

Jesus assigned team roles to His apostles. Here are a few.
1.  Peter, James, John (Personal Assistants and Companions to Jesus), Matthew 17:1.
2.  Judas (Treasurer), John 12:6.
3.  Philip (Food Service Manager), John 6:5-6.

Jesus was careful to select those who fit their unique abilities. If you are a professional soccer coach, you would not place a four-foot-tall player as your goalie, regardless of their passion for the position. Conversely, you would not assign an athlete the position who hates playing it.

Nehemiah mastered the art of designating roles when rebuilding the old Jerusalem wall. I imagine his initial team meeting went something like this:

"Eliashib and you other priests, get to the Sheep Gate! Start fixing the doors! Get some help from the citizens of Jericho. They've got nothing better to do!"

"Hey, sons of Hassenaah! Lay out some beams and get those doors going! Don't forget to bolt them in tight! Meremoth and your crew work on the section next to Hassenaah's kids!"

"What? Hey, Tekoa people...You refuse to work with the supervisors? Knock off the attitude and get busy!"

"Good job, Joiada and Meshullam! Way to get that Old City Gate up! Hey, Harhaiah and Hananiah, good job fortifying that section of Jerusalem. This is nothing like your old jobs of designing jewelry and making perfumes, right?"

It is important to establish roles on the team that fit people's passions and skills. Your team is likely to be mostly (or entirely) volunteers. People who are assigned roles not fitting their passions rarely stay for long. People stay around if they are excited about the future and contribute in a manner they love.

But beware of a common trap. Many leaders have developed skills in areas they do not enjoy. Training people to do what they hate is a losing game. They will resent you and eventually leave. Until that time, they will become a detrimental influence on the team.

## T.E.A.M.

There are too many acronyms in the W.O.R.L.D. In thinkSMALL Ministries, we created an (get-ready) 'acronym' for the steps Jesus used to manage His team: T.E.A.M.

Jesus' approach was revolutionary, and his words were transformational. His leadership methods left a lasting impact on his followers and continue to provide timeless lessons for leaders today.

### T = Training

*16 "All Scripture is inspired by God and is useful to teach us what is true and to make us realize what is wrong in our lives. It corrects us when we are wrong and teaches us to do what is right. 17 God uses it to prepare and equip his people to do every good work" (2 Timothy 3:16-17).*

Jesus trained His team for three years. There is no substitute for teams well-prepared to win.

Train (T) your team with scripture, prayer, modeling and practice.

## E = Equip/Empower/Encourage

*24 "Let us think of ways to motivate one another to acts of love and good works"* (Hebrews 10:24).

Jesus' team was well equipped with scripture and knowledge. Jesus empowered His team with scripture and prayer. He encouraged and taught them to encourage one another toward 'love and good works.'

Empower, Equip, and Encourage (E) your team with spiritual strength, practical ideas, and faith-building encouragement.

## A = Accompany

*4 Jesus[a] knew the Pharisees had heard that he was baptizing and making more disciples than John 2 (though Jesus himself didn't baptize them—his disciples did) (John 4:1-2)*

This is one of the most important aspects of Jesus' training. Jesus did not train and release others to ministry. He stuck around. I imagine Jesus relaxing by the shore sipping tea while His apostles dunked new believers into the Jordan. "Peter!" Jesus might have yelled "Let the guy up! You want him to drown?!"

Jesus accompanied His team, encouraging and correcting them until they were ready to be sent out.

The corporate world assigns this role to a quality control manager. A seasoned and skilled leader will watch people perform the activities, review their successes, and correct their errors. Since people are in the learning stage, their confidence may be low. Over-emphasize what they are doing well. Under-emphasize what they are doing poorly. Always encourage.

Use the sandwich approach for any corrections. Surround the 'negative' meat with two 'positive' slices of bread.

"Peter, I'm really impressed by your enthusiasm" (positive).

"Sadly, you held the person under the water too long, and he drowned" (negative).

"However, I believe that you are only one step away from having people live through the experience of baptism. Well done!" (positive).

Accompany your team and watch for ways to encourage and correct them until they can be effective without you.

### M = Mobilize, Mentor

In John MacArthur's book *12 Ordinary Men*, he writes about when Jesus selected and sent out 72 disciples: "Jesus Christ teamed them in pairs so that they would offer one another mutual support. Throughout this phase of their training, the Lord Himself stuck closely with them. He was like a mother eagle, watching the eaglets as they began to fly. They were always checking back with Him, reporting on how things were going (cf. Luke 9:10; 10:17). And after a couple of seasons of evangelistic labor, they returned to the Lord and remained with Him for an extended time of teaching, ministry, fellowship, and rest" (Mark 6:30-34).

When they returned to Jesus they were fired up! *"Lord, even the demons submit to us in Your name!"* (Luke 10:17).

They must have been waiting for Jesus' to celebrate with them. He might have. But then it was time for some perspective. He said *"… do not rejoice that the spirits submit to you, but rejoice that your names are written in heaven"* (Luke 10:20).

Not to rain on their parade, Jesus was always there to remind them of the highest priorities, the vision. A great leader always does.

Jesus promised that His mentorship would be eternal.

*26 "But when the Father sends the Advocate as my representative— that is, the Holy Spirit—he will teach you everything and will remind you of everything I have told you* (John 14:26).

Equip your team with experienced mentors they respect. They will keep the vision alive, the priorities in place, and the team encouraged. Coach your mentors to not yield to the temptation to overcontrol the ministry. The mentor can coach, listen, and advise but the youth must be trusted to lead. Through their leadership experience and successful outcomes, more of them will hear the voice of God leading them into future ministry leadership.

Mobilize and mentor your team consistently. They will need leadership encouragement when they fall short of their goals and guidance to point them back in the right direction. Consistent feedback keeps your team spiritually and missionally on track!

A well-trained visionary team empowered with scripture and led by a confident and encouraging leader can reach great heights. As the leader exhibits and teaches the ways of Christ, the team learns to encourage, pray and motivate one another. Their confidence will grow, with success a natural outcome. They will grow closer to Christ together.

*20 "My prayer is not for them alone. I pray also for those who will believe in me through their message, 21 that all of them may be one, Father, just as you are in me and I am in you. May they also be in us so that the world may believe that you have sent me. 22 I have given them the glory that you gave me, that they may be one as we are one— 23 I in them and you in me—so that they may be brought to complete unity. Then the world will know that you sent me and have loved them even as you have loved me." John 17:20-23*

"When you go out into the world, watch out for traffic, hold hands, and stick together." (Robert Fulghum, *All I Really Need to Know I Learned in Kindergarten*).

## THE POWER OF EARLY SUCCESS

As previously mentioned, for most people confidence stems from success. (How confident were you before you gave your first awesome sermon)? Ensure your team experiences success early on!

When Jesus sent out His 72 disciples, He gave them simple goals: share the Gospel and report back to Him. These goals required a bit of effort but nobody was unable to do them. And when they returned, they felt they had succeeded. Their confidence grew. (Of course, a future more challenging goal was coming; to make disciples of every nation in the world. It was probably best that he didn't start with that one!).

"You earn confidence by success". (Pete Carrol, NFL Coach)

Early success creates confidence and momentum. Immediate failure produces death.

Here are 2 things to teach your team:

1. All efforts are successful.
2. Failure is an essential part of success.

One of the most important lessons I've learned is to prepare the team to succeed on the first try! Look for things they did well and celebrate them highly! Your first goal is to inspire confidence so they can continue. Don't ignore the mistakes, but mainly emphasize the effort! Over time, they will improve. If you lose them in the early stages, you may not get them back.

### KEEP IN MIND:

1. Choose leaders who exhibit gratitude, humility, and a passion for the mission; these qualities promote dedication and productive leadership.

2. Assign team responsibilities according to each member's interests and abilities to guarantee ongoing participation and positive impact on the team.

3. Follow Jesus' leadership process of T (train), E (Equip), A (Accompany), M (Mobilize/Mentor) to ensure success

Don't make the mistake of catching fish only to have them jump back into the water! In the next chapter, we'll review some keys to providing a church experience so powerful children will never think to leave!

## CHAPTER 14

# KEEPING FISH IN THE BOAT: REVERSING THE EXODUS OF KIDS FROM CHURCH

*"Start children off on the way they should go, and even when they are old they will not turn from it."*
— Proverbs 22:6

I hate to disagree with someone as wise as Solomon. Perhaps 3,000 years ago, children had a better track record. Sometimes, it seems "the way they should go" is right out the door! It's a global phenomenon. The exodus. It's in Boston and Bangkok, in Nashville and Nairobi. Children and youth are leaving. Around the world, pastors are witnessing the steady decline of young people in church. Most of them do not have an effective plan. That is what this chapter is about.

The exodus of children has long-reaching effects. An increasing number of pastors wonder who will become their future leaders.

Barna Group states "Pastors believe it's harder now than before to find mature young Christians who want to become pastors." Seventy-eight percent are concerned about the quality of future Christian leaders.[36]

In 2011, David Kinnaman (CEO Barna Group) reported in his book "You Lost Me" that 59 percent of children in the US dropped out of church after age 15. In 2019, that number increased to 64 percent.[37]

They are leaving earlier than ever. Do you doubt it? Compare the number of primary school children in your church to the number of high school students. If children outnumber high school students, you have likely experienced an exodus. Moses would be proud. But it is one of the greatest threats to the health and future of the local church.

Culture is draining your pool of future leaders.

## WHY DO KIDS LEAVE?

It's annoying to pull a fish into the boat, turn your back, and hear the splash as it jumps back into the water.

Most children leave church in their middle school years. Why is that? Is it culture? Peer pressure? And what role do parents play in this?

In too many churches, kids go through this cycle: They worship. They learn. They play. They pray. And then they leave. Why? In 2011, the Barna Group conducted a study to answer that question.[38]

Despite what you may have guessed, here are three responses that did not make the list of reasons:

---

[36] Barna Research, The State of Pastors Volume 2

[37] David Kinnaman, Faith for Exiles: 5 Ways for a New Generation to Follow Jesus in Digital Babylon

[38] Barna Group, 2011 Barna 59% Six Reasons Young Christians Leave Church; https://www.barna.com/research/six-reasons-young-christians-leave-church/

- My Sunday School teacher was not fun enough.
- My church did not have good enough snacks.
- My church did not have a climbing wall.

Let's debunk a few common myths.

Myth #1: "The exodus of young people is due to college influence."

(Most kids leave church before college.)

Myth #2: "It's a normal part of the maturing process."

(If this were true, why do 40 percent of kids decide to stay in church? Are they abnormal?)

Myth #3: "Children are Biblically illiterate."

(Studies show that children's Biblical literacy in 2024 is approximately the same as in 1950).

Myth #4: "They will eventually come back."

(This may be the biggest myth of all. Only about 30% of teens who leave church ever return).[39]

## THE 4 R'S

If we understand why children leave, we can build strategies to reverse the trend. Let's discuss four of the most common reasons, each beginning with the letter R. Each one connects to questions buried deep within a child's subconscious mind.

## THE FIRST R: RELATIONSHIPS

A child wonders, "Are my relational needs being met in my church experience?"

---

[39] Lifeway Research, Most Teenagers Drop Out of Church When They Become Young Adults; https://research.lifeway.com/2019/01/15/most-teenagers-drop-out-of-church-as-young-adults/

Children's emotional security is linked to relationships. As essential as air, they seek feelings of love and acceptance.

Children require relationships that stretch from a personal connection with Jesus to engagement with the entire church. Kids spend about one hour a week in church, but 30 to 50 hours a week with children in school or their neighborhood. Children whose closest friends are in church want to spend time together during the week. Without them, non-Christian peers can draw them away.

## THE SECOND R: RELEVANCE

A child wonders, "Is the church helping me solve my Monday through Saturday issues?" One of the most common reasons given by children who leave church is that the teaching is no longer relevant to their daily lives.

Children do not discount the importance of prayer, but feel the church falls short in helping them deal with issues affecting their non-spiritual lives.

Children between the ages of 12 to 15 are experiencing puberty, social insecurities, peer pressure, and perhaps the temptation of drugs or pornography. They are not sure how to deal with social media, their sexual drives, or identities. Middle-school-aged kids are transitioning to a more independent life.

To a middle school child, churches are irrelevant if they lack an environment to discuss the problematic social issues of the day.

## THE THIRD R: RESPONSIBILITY

A child wonders, "Am I important to the church and its mission?"

Most parents know that assigning tasks for children increases their sense of personal value and purpose.

Churches that fail to give children opportunities to be valued contributors are likely to lose them.

## THE FOURTH R: REASON

A child wonders, "How can I make sense of it all?"

*Pseudoscience: a system of theories, assumptions, and methods errone-ously regarded as scientific* (Merriam-Webster Dictionary).

Many teachers use socially rooted or pseudoscientific arguments to try to sway children's beliefs about God and the divinity of Jesus.

Children trust adults. Parents teach children to believe their teachers. Yet even after attending church for years, a child's faith can be shaken easily if unprepared.

Most non-Christian school teachers are well-meaning, even those who attempt to sway our children from Christ. Most were victims of pseudoscientific indoctrination by secular college professors. These students become teachers who bring this wonky logic to children who (unless trained) buy it 'hook, line, and sinker.'

*It is time to secure children deeply for Christ, guide them into a full and joyous life and empower them to stay the course so no one will 'snatch them out of His hand.'* (John 10:28).

## SOLUTIONS: TURNING IT ALL AROUND

Let's look at some ideas you can implement in your church. Some of them may be a perfect fit. Some may not. You may come up with your own. You and your leadership team must determine the strategies that best equip your children spiritually and practically. The best decision you can make is to begin the process immediately!

**RELATIONSHIPS:** How can your church begin to help kids deepen their relationships with Jesus, other kids, youth, and the over-all church?

1. Jesus

How deep does your discipleship curriculum go in training children to engage Jesus on a personal level? Do children pray exclusively by rote? Do they maintain an ongoing connection with Him in their daily lives?

*"Here I am! I stand at the door and knock. If anyone hears my voice and opens the door, I will come in and eat with that person, and they with me"* (Revelation 3:20).

Ideas: Talk with your children's teachers. Examine your current discipleship materials. If they are limited to only Bible stories and games, supplement them with a relational-oriented curriculum!

Encourage children to visit hospitals, retirement homes, and Christian homeless shelters to foster meaningful relationships. At a young age, show them how God can use them to be a spiritual blessing to others.

## 2. Other Kids

Does your church guide and assist children to pray for one another on a one on one basis? Are they taught what God says about the power of their prayers (Psalm 8:2, Matthew 21:14-16)?

*Through the praise of children and infants you have established a stronghold against your enemies, to silence the foe and the avenger* (Psalm 8:2).

Ideas: Train children and assist them in praying for one another individually and collectively. Find games and activities designed to help children make new friends in church. Choose activities that can spiritually deepen relationships, ensuring that friendships made in church are more meaningful than those with non-believing children. Provide local field trips for church kids to ballgames, parks, hiking, etc.

## 3. Youth

Are your youth connected to children? In most churches, there is a relationship gap between high school and middle school kids.

Children look up to the ones slightly older. And the older ones can help steer them through the difficult middle school age times.

Ideas: Find ways to inspire your high school group to establish relationships and mentor middle school students. Use similar strat-egies to link middle school students with primary school children. This process will not only help reduce the departure of children but also help cultivate future leaders!

## 4. Church

Do you connect your kids to the general body of the church? Is it possible they feel alienated from the adults? Are you unintentionally making them feel 'unqualified' to serve an important role? Do they feel less valuable than others?

Ideas: Look to strengthen the relationships between children and the church. Introduce staff members on a rotating basis to children in church. Have them share their church responsibilities with kids and encourage them to ask questions. Find time to eat, play, and pray with them.

**RELEVANCE:** How can you make church more relevant to kids' Monday through Saturday lives?

Does your church ask children what concerns them in their daily lives? What pressures are they under? How do they feel about the internet, social media, drugs, gender identity, sexual temptations? What unique issues or problems cause them stress?

Ideas: Teach kids how Biblical principles apply to real-world is-sues. How can you help them deal with peer pressure, relationships, social media, identity and more? Open the floor to open discussions. Make your church a welcoming, judgment-free place where kids can discuss issues, regardless of sensitivities. Mobilize your youth team and connect them with the children!

Kids will look for answers to these questions with friends and teachers if not provided in the church.

**RESPONSIBILITY**: How can your church give kids more responsibility?

Does your church provide responsibilities for the children?

Ideas: Allow children to do some tasks currently led by adults. Make them assistant greeters. Let them serve coffee. Assign them to lead adults to their seats. Choose one of them to bring water or sermon notes to the pastor. Give them responsibility to write the bulletin (even if it is in crayon or colored pencils). Teach them how to share Bible lessons to their peers or 'younger' kids. Allow them occasionally to share testimonies with the congregation. Occasionally, give them a microphone. Show them the respect they deserve.

*...He said to them, "Let the children come to me. Don't stop them!...*" (Mark 10:14).

Here's a challenge: Occasionally, let a primary or middle school-aged child give a sermon.    When you empower children with significant responsibilities, you strengthen their character. They feel you trust them, honor them. Their natural response is to do the same for you. They recognize they have an essential role in the church and are far more likely to stay.

**REASON:** How can your church help kids defend their faith to non-believers?

*"...Always be prepared to give an answer to everyone who asks you to give the reason for the hope that you have..."* (1 Peter 3:15).

Many churches have a child-apologetics curriculum. Yet most of them are exclusive to scripture. The problem is that when children go to school, teachers do not use scripture to question Christianity. They lean on a type of logic that an untrained child cannot easily debate.

A child can defeat pseudoscience or shaky logic if prepared. Are you preparing them?

*16 "Look, I am sending you out as sheep among wolves. So be as shrewd as snakes and harmless as doves."* (Matthew 10:16)

Would you send an unarmed soldier into battle? Do children have to subjugate logic to hold onto faith?

As children enter public schools, they are vulnerable to arguments that seem reasonable to a young, unprepared mind. Non-Christian teachers and friends have their attention. Their arguments against Christianity are rooted in pseudo-logic, philosophy, feelings, or unsupported science. They are defeatable but to accomplish that mission, children are best prepared with scripture and logic.

If a child's faith hangs entirely on scripture, they are vulnerable. Peter understood that 'reason' is compatible with God's words. A child not equipped to respond to challenges with a spiritual and logical mindset is not fully armed and can begin to doubt their faith.

Do not underestimate the ability of young children to learn how to respond to basic statements and questions such as these;

1. Jesus was not a real person.
2. If God loves the world, why does He allow evil to exist?
3. Is there evidence to support the resurrection?
4. What reason is there to believe in miracles?
5. A Supreme Being did not create the world.
6. Human beings evolved from bacteria and primitive animals.
7. God made some boys in girls bodies, and vice versa.

Ideas: Seek out Christian child apologetics that strengthens the logical side of a child's brain. Authors including Lee Strobel and J. Warner Wallace have stepped into this arena. Check out *Mama Bear Apologetics* by Hillary Morgan Ferrer or other materials online. Do not shirk from the responsibility to arm your children in this way. They will benefit from understanding the logical aspects of God and their faith will grow! Help your children to put on every armor of God to defend their faith!

*14 "Then we will no longer be infants, tossed back and forth by the waves, and blown here and there by every wind of teaching and by the cunning and craftiness of people in their deceitful scheming* (Ephesians 4:14).

With the proper tools and strategies, you can win the war against children, empower them, help your church regain its future, and become the transformational agent God intends it to be.

## ROLES (OF PARENTS):

Pastors are increasingly concerned about parents' lack of involvement in discipling their children. According to Barna Group[40], less than 10 percent of Christian parents actively disciple their children at home. And yet, who gets the blame when church attending children go 'off the rails' when they reach their teen years? (I think you know.)

Children attend Sunday school for about one hour a week in most churches. A typical church may have one Sunday school teacher for every ten children. In this scenario, if a teacher could divide their hours equally among the kids, each child would receive only six minutes of personal time per week. However, even this example isn't possible, as there is little time for personal one-on-one attention in church. Ideas: Many parents are willing to disciple their children but feel ill-equipped. Hold parents discipleship meetings. Share curriculum with them. Train them how to use it at home. Teach them how

---

40  Arizona Christian University, Most US Parents Have No Plan for Kids' Spiritual Development, Research Finds;
https://www.arizonachristian.edu/2023/09/06/most-us-parents-have-no-plan-for-kids-spiritual-development/

to pray with their children. Let them know the responsibility given to them, and the relational and spiritual benefits of being directly involved in discipleship. Make sure the fathers, in particular, understand their role.

*⁴"Fathers, do not provoke your children to anger by the way you treat them. Rather, bring them up with the discipline and instruction that comes from the Lord"* (Ephesians 6:4).

## ARE YOUTH WILLING TO RETURN?

Over the past 20 years, churches have increasingly watched young people leave church. Barna Group discovered that most reasons centered around judgmental and irrelevant church culture.[41] Many churches responded by changing their worship and teaching to a younger style that appealed more to the youth in the community. However, they lost some of their older congregants who were vital financial contributors to the church.

Some long-established church youth felt the changes were compromising and eventually left. The Barna survey asked young people why, and 31 percent claimed "church is boring. 23 percent said "the Bible is not taught clearly or often enough." 20 percent stated "God seems missing from my experience of church."

Then the COVID pandemic hit. People, including young people, began asking the right questions. "What is life about? I am here for a reason? Is there an eternal plan? Does God exist? Can science and religion coexist?" The strange dichotomy is that while many churches shifted to reach a more secularized youth culture, the secularized youth started becoming more spiritual.[42]

---

[41] Barna Group, 2011 Barna 59% Six Reasons Young Christians Leave Church; https://www.barna.com/research/six-reasons-young-christians-leave-church/

[42] Barna Group, Over Half of Gen Z Teens Feel Motivated to Learn More About Jesus; https://www.barna.com/research/teens-and-jesus/

Today's youth are truth seekers. Increasingly they perceive the existence of a higher power and have a stronger desire to understand Who He is and how to worship Him. Churches that teach the divinity of God's Word, respect science and logic, allow a more expressive worship style, and empower them with responsibility will win them over.

## WESTSIDE CHRISTIAN FELLOWSHIP

Pastor Shane Idleman leads Westside Christian Fellowship in Lancaster, California. He witnessed youth and children increasingly disappear from church and was motivated to understand why.

Shane interviewed some of these young people and asked why they had moved on. The most common reasons were that they felt the church became irrelevant to their lives, overly judgmental, or disconnected from their struggles.

Then it got personal. Teenagers told him the worship music was uninspiring, and his unrelatable sermons were tailored to the older generations who represented most of the church. They believed the church failed to meet their need for a deeper connection with God.

Shane was at a crossroads. He could hold firm and maintain the ways his church had traditionally operated, or he could adjust. He was aware that big changes would make some adults uncomfortable or possibly make them want to leave the church. He needed to figure out how to strike the optimum balance between generations. The future of his church was on the line. He and his staff sprang into action! They modified the music with the aid of their youth to provide deeper worship experiences across all age groups. Pastor Shane added fresh, Biblically-based sermons that offered practical solutions for problems young people experienced daily. Nothing was off-limits, including mental health, drugs, social media, and sexual identity.

The church reformulated its youth ministry and introduced more relevant lessons and activities. They empowered their young leaders to facilitate youth-oriented discussion events on weeknights to draw in more young people.

Pastor Shane's team collaborated with youth leaders to launch new community outreach initiatives, sparking excitement and boosting young people's passion for church leadership.    Pastor Shane also strengthened his congregation's commitment to cross-generational fellowship and mentorship. He encouraged adults to mentor youth, resulting in intergenerational relationships that delivered guidance and encouragement.

Westside Christian Fellowship revitalized and fortified its youth ministry, creating a framework to ensure the next generation of youth will value the church. It is a fantastic example of a church stepping in to prevent a possible disaster.

Establish a church environment where children and youth would never want to leave!

## KEEP IN MIND:

1. 64 percent of children leave church in their teen years—and only 30 percent ever return.

2. Relationships, relevance, responsibility, and reason are key reasons why children leave. Strategies that address each issue can stop the exodus from your church.

3. Parents play a critical role in discipling kids but often lack tools and encouragement.

## CHAPTER 15

# SETTING SAIL: CASTING OFF FOR A WHOLE NEW FUTURE

*"See, I am doing a new thing!"*
—Isaiah 43:19

"God provides the wind, Man must raise the sail."
—Saint Augustine, 354-430

The weather is perfect. The morning sun is rising, peeking its orange head just above the hills. There's a breeze from the southeast, and a gentle current on the water. You've loaded your boat with the finest rods, nets and bait. You've even remembered the sandwiches. You have identified the fishing spot where they are hungrily awaiting your arrival. You've charted your course. All you need to do is push off and raise your sail.

It wasn't easy getting up at 5 a.m. this morning. Sleeping in was an option—so many do—but you are different. While others trade opportunities for rest, you embrace it. You do not belong to the army of Ephraim but the courageous and committed army of God.

⁹ *The men of Ephraim, though armed with bows, turned back on the day of battle;* (Psalm 78:9).

You are not this way.

## DELEGATE, BUT DON'T HESITATE

*"If not us, who? If not now, when?"* President John Fitzgerald Kennedy.

Perhaps you are like me. Daily activities become a stranglehold. It is difficult to find time to do what is essential. Additionally, my nature is to procrastinate. I've been putting off telling you this (bad joke).

Begin now. Lead or delegate what you have learned, but don't delay. If you wait over three days to begin, you will likely not act. What you have learned will fade and the future of your church will not change.

In the church of Fleeting Assurance, where sermons once inspired,

A pastor with good intentions was overworked and tired.

"I'll get to it tomorrow," he'd often say with pride,

But tomorrow turned to yesterday, for he knew inside he'd lied.

One day at his pulpit, he gazed upon the place,

His church had lost its young ones, gone without a trace.

The congregation smaller, regret now filled his eyes,

As he remembered glad hellos, replaced with silent goodbyes.

## NEXT STEPS

Decide now to save your church's future. Review, refresh, and resell its vision to your congregation. Assess the gap between where you are and where you want to be, and choose a strategy to grow your church today and tomorrow. Gather and empower your youth to lead social ministry on behalf of children. Fill the gap between both generations to create a powerful force for the future.

Choose community-connection strategies that are unique to your church and Great Commission-focused. Set written team goals that are possible yet challenge all team members

Disciple children in a way that deepens their relationship with Jesus, each other, and the church. Don't hide them in their rooms but mobilize them in important church roles. Lead them to do ministry within the community. Arm them with the tools to defend their faith in school with scripture, science, and logic.

The minnows are hungry and swimming next to your boat. Throw your net.

It's time to fish.

# MEET THE AUTHOR

Rev. Gary Hays is the founder and President of thinkSMALL Ministries, serving over 3,000 churches in 20 nations. Through his ministry, thinkSmall, over 1.4 million people have come to Christ, with more than 70% entering into long-term discipleship.

Gary specializes in teaching pastors how to use Jesus' lesser-known strategies to grow their church, develop future leaders, and ensure long-term sustainability. He is a skilled vision-caster encouraging leaders toward youth mobilization and child evangelism.

Gary, an ordained minister, has spoken at churches, and conferences in 17 countries across Asia, Africa, Latin America and the USA.

Gary served four years in the Air Force during the Vietnam War, working in military intelligence with a Top Secret Security Clearance. He later studied at the University of Washington, launched a successful import business, and became a national manager for a global food company.

In 2005, Gary and Paula left corporate life, sold their home, and became missionaries in Thailand, founding thinkSMALL in 2007. They now direct the ministry from the United States.

Gary has written numerous training resources for churches including Transforming Nations Through Children, The Four Callings of Jesus, Biblical Goal Setting, Eradicating Trafficking Through the Local Church, Jesus-Style Leadership, Strategic Planning for Churches, and Reversing the Exodus (How to Keep Children in Church).

He currently lives with his wonderful wife Paula in Phoenix, Arizona.

www.ingramcontent.com/pod-product-compliance
Lightning Source LLC
Chambersburg PA
CBHW051141120626
46547CB00012B/899